Screening Shakespeare
Using Film to Understand the Plays

Michael Greer

PEARSON

Longman

New York Boston San Francisco
London Toronto Sydney Tokyo Singapore Madrid
Mexico City Munich Paris Cape Town Hong Kong Montreal

Cover Image:
Joseph Fiennes in *Shakespeare in Love* (1998) dir. John Madden
Miramax Films/Universal Pictures / The Kobal Collection
Photographer: Laurie Sparham

Greer, *Screening Shakespeare: Using Film to Understand the Plays*

Copyright ©2004 Pearson Education, Inc.

ISBN: 0-321-19479-9

1 2 3 4 5 6 7 8 9 10–CRW–06 05 04 03

Contents

PREFACE

Screening Shakespeare is designed to be used in tandem with David Bevington's edition of *The Complete Works of Shakespeare* (5th ed., Longman, 2004). It can be used with any edition of Shakespeare's works, but makes specific references to, and draws upon, the approach outlined in Bevington's editorial introductions. It is written primarily for college audiences, specifically students taking a major author course in Shakespeare and studying his works in depth for the first time.

Screening Shakespeare proposes that using film empowers students to see themselves as interpreters, providing a foundation for working with the complex language and historical contexts of the plays. It is written in an accessible style and its practical approach gives students analytical tools and rubrics for engaging film without overwhelming them with terminology or theory. By treating films as cultural texts, it encourages students to go beyond questions of plot and form to seriously consider the historical impact of Shakespeare on our culture as well as the impact of our culture on Shakespeare.

I've followed the basic outline of Bevington's anthology, dividing the plays by genre, beginning with the comedies and continuing through the histories and tragedies. Within each genre, the plays are treated in the order they were written (as far as we have been able to date them). This allows readers to see how Shakespeare's development of certain themes, sources, and story lines evolve over time.

My approach to each play is framed by the comments and themes presented in David Bevington's introductions. His editorial introductions to each work identify key themes, sources, structural elements, and critical issues in the plays. I find the individual introductions to be valuable starting points, and I tend to return to them when working with films based on a specific play. Like these introductions, the discussions of specific films in *Screening Shakespeare* are meant to be suggestive rather than definitive. Their goal is to pose useful and interesting questions about the films that readers can develop further in their own writing and classroom discussions.

Many of the existing books on Shakespeare films offer extensive reviews and critical commentary on the merits of particular films. *Screening Shakespeare* generally does not offer such evaluations. For readers who are relatively new to Shakespeare's plays, almost any film can be helpful and interesting and can shed light on the plot, themes, and dialogue of the play. The point is to use the films creatively to ask interesting and fruitful questions about the plays and the issues surrounding them. My practice is to ask lots of questions and to suggest an inquiry-based approach to the films that, ideally, will lead readers back to the plays with new insight and renewed energy.

HOW TO USE THIS BOOK

Screening Shakespeare is designed to help readers use film and video to better understand and appreciate Shakespeare's plays. Whether you are struggling to understand the language or looking for additional insight into a play you already know well, taking the time to watch a filmed version of a play can be a helpful strategy for learning more about Shakespeare's works. This guide is intended to give you some critical insight and analytical tools to use in conjunction with your experience of the films, in order to make you a more informed, confident, and accomplished reader of the plays.

Screening Shakespeare can be used for independent study or in-class discussion. Some instructors will assign films and spend time discussing, viewing, and responding to them in class. The questions provided in this guide can be used in large- or small-group discussions. They may provide some ideas for group or individual presentations if you are expected to prepare a report for your class about a particular film. The questions are also written to serve as potential writing prompts or topics for both formal and informal writing projects.

Students can also use this book in the context of individual study. Even if your instructor does not plan to spend class time on the films, you may find it helpful to watch some of them in preparation for class discussion. The films aren't really a *substitute* for carefully reading the text of the plays because filmmakers almost always cut and rearrange scenes in order to make them work on the screen. Entire scenes, key speeches, and even whole characters may be edited out of a film version of a Shakespeare play, so be careful not to rely exclusively on the films if you want to be successful in your Shakespeare course.

Many Shakespeare instructors and scholars do agree, though, that watching films *in conjunction with* reading the text can be a very productive way to approach and engage one of the plays. If you read David Bevington's introductions to each play, for example, you'll notice that he often comments on recent film versions of the play being introduced. Most Shakespeare teachers tend to be avid fans of theater and film, and they recognize the value of both for their students.

Chapter 1 provides a framework and some basic concepts for analyzing film. It maps out the kinds of questions and the type or critical analysis I find useful in viewing films based on Shakespeare's plays. It's probably a good idea to read through chapter 1 before moving on to specific films in later chapters. Otherwise, it's possible to pick and choose among discussions of specific films in any order. I don't expect many readers to sit down and tackle *Screening Shakespeare* cover to cover. I've designed it to be useful to readers who want to locate background and questions about a specific film quickly.

Here's a strategy you might use for watching a film and reading the text in a "multimedia approach" to one of the plays. Start by reading Bevington's introduction to the play in your *Complete Works*. This will introduce you to the form of the play, its literary and historical sources, and give you some ideas of what to watch for. Then read through the play once, forging ahead to get the basic sense of the dramatic action without getting too bogged down in the details. Skip over sections of dialogue that don't make sense at first. Review the play by looking at the *Dramatis Personae* at its beginning. Review the list of characters and see if you remember something about each of the main characters and what they say and do.

Now you should be ready to watch the film and respond to it as an informed and critical viewer. Watch the film straight through on a first viewing. You may want to jot down brief notes about anything that you notice that strikes you as especially interesting or unusual about the film. Whatever stands out as interesting or creative (or even confusing) might provide a productive starting point for a discussion or an essay about a film. Write your thoughts down so you can remember them the next day in class and later.

If you have time, it can be especially useful to go back and review specific scenes to reinforce them in your memory. Our visual memories do not last very long, so make detailed notes about how a scene looks when you have the film in front of you. Read the lines in the text, then watch the scene on-screen, and so forth. DVD is an especially efficient format for jumping from scene to scene, using the scene menu function. Some of the films discussed in this guide are available only on VHS, which makes this process a little more tedious, but it's still possible using the cue/review function.

Once you have worked through the film a second time and written more detailed notes about it, you'll probably find that the words virtually jump off the page when you go back to reread the text of the play. On a first reading, you may find it hard to connect the words on the page to the dramatic action and events taking place on the stage. Once you've watched the play on film, though, you'll find that you remember character's accents, the rhythm and emotion they used to emphasize certain words, phrases, and lines, and so forth. You'll be able to visualize what is happening in a certain scene. You'll discover that a text that seemed static and difficult, perhaps even impenetrable, has suddenly opened up and become meaningful for you.

For each play covered in this guide, I've provided some background, discussion questions, and specific analysis. Compare these sections with your own notes and responses to the film(s). Maybe you notice things that aren't discussed in this book, or maybe something discussed here will trigger new insights for you. Shakespeare's plays can be interpreted and visualized in multiple ways, and there is no single correct meaning for any play or speech. The best interpretations are the ones that help you understand the text and which help you to explain what is happening in a play and why.

Chapter 5 and the additional resources in the back of this book suggest some further ideas for reading, viewing, and writing about Shakespeare films. There are many ways to study film, from a formal standpoint, through the lenses of critical theory, or in the context of popular culture. The approach you take will be shaped by your own prior experience with film and by the context of your class and the perspectives it provides.

It's my conviction that learning and having fun with Shakespeare should be interconnected processes, and I hope *Screening Shakespeare* offers some ideas and strategies that enable you to better understand and enjoy both the films and the plays.

CHAPTER 1

Shakespeare on Film

The Internet Movie Database lists more than 500 films based on or adapted from the works of William Shakespeare. This number includes international and made-for-TV films in addition to feature films, but it's still an impressive figure. Shakespeare has been translated into film since the very infancy of film as a medium. The earliest known Shakespeare film dates from 1899, starring English actor Herbert Beerbohm Tree in a three-minute silent version of a scene from *King John*. Since that time, *Hamlet* has been filmed more than 90 times, *Macbeth* 50, and *Romeo and Juliet* 40 times. Shakespeare's plays have been filmed in more than 20 languages and in at least that many different countries. The plays continue to be adapted and reinvented in new settings and genres. Recent film adaptations include *King Rikki*, a 2002 film advertised as "Shakespeare's *Richard III* in 21st Century Los Angeles"; *O*, a 2001 adaptation of *Othello*, in which the main character is a star player on the high school basketball team instead of a military general; and *Scotland, Pa.* (2001), which rewrites *Macbeth* as a black comedy, featuring Joe "Mac" McBeth, a fry cook with an ambitious wife who prods him on to kill his boss in a plot to take over the local fast food joint.

It's hard to imagine any other literary author who has had such a long-standing influence on Anglo-American and world cinema. By way of comparison, novelist Charles Dickens, for example, has been translated into film 168 times; mystery writer Agatha Christie, 78. Stephen King, the English language's all-time best-selling author, has also been adapted for the screen 78 times. (Again, these numbers are based on information obtained from *The Internet Movie Database*.) Even these well-known and popular authors apparently do not even approach Shakespeare in terms of their cinematic productivity. The popular English playwright of the Elizabethan era appears to have a highly successful second career in our time as a screenwriter.

Alongside the films themselves, we find a small but growing body of scholarly and critical work on Shakespearean cinema. (Selected critical works are listed in the additional resources at the back of this book.) We now have at least one major book-length history of Shakespeare on screen (Rothwell), one critical study intended for undergraduate courses (Cartmell), and two substantial essay collections covering various dimensions of the films (Davies and Wells; Jackson). Most of this scholarly output has been published since 1994, indicating that the study of Shakespeare on film remains a young and informal subfield within Shakespeare studies, but one significant book did appear as early as 1977 (Jorgens). There may still be some debate about whether or not Shakespeare on film counts as a substantial component of Shakespeare studies, but it is clear that a growing number of scholars are taking film seriously as a medium for teaching and interpreting the plays. Performance theory and cultural studies have helped shift attention from the texts themselves toward performance and popular culture, providing a context and a rationale for continued serious study of the films.

What can we discover by taking the time to watch, discuss, and write about all these Shakespeare movies? What can be learned from a film that couldn't better be learned from sustained study of a play's printed text? Why, if you already have to read and learn a dozen or more new plays in a semester, might you want to spend even more time renting and watching four *Hamlet* films or two *Romeo and Juliets*?

My first answer is that watching a film can help you better understand and appreciate what's going on in the text of a play. It's often difficult to read the printed text and visualize what's happening during a given speech or scene. A film provides a sense of setting, dramatic action, and context that often can be hard to extract from a literal reading of the text of a play. You can see the actors' expressions, read their nonverbal cues and body language as they speak (or listen, or react), and begin to see the dynamics of their relationships and the conflicts that drive the plot. Occasionally, Shakespeare readers can get bogged down in trying to ferret out the literal sense of a line or scene and lose sight of the plot or the dramatic context. Watching a film of the same scene can help you see and hear what's happening and how it fits into the larger dramatic patterns of the play, even if you still don't know exactly, literally, what the lines mean. Hearing a good actor recite a speech can provide meaning in the form of tone, inflection, rhythm, and gesture that will help you get more out of the words when you return to the text later.

We know that Shakespeare wrote his plays to be performed and that he did not even bother to publish them as printed works in his own lifetime. He evidently saw their meaning and significance on the stage in live performance rather than on the page as works of literature. If you have opportunities to see live theatrical performances on campus or in a local Shakespeare festival, by all means do so. There's no substitute for live performances to bring the plays to life in every sense of the word. But it's unlikely that you'll be able to find live performances for every play you want to read and study. So the films, on VHS or DVD, provide a viable alternative. They can help you see how a play might be performed, how its setting might look, what costumes the actors might wear, what kind of music might accompany the dramatic action, and so forth.

If you're studying Shakespeare in a formal college course setting (as I imagine most of my readers are), you're probably aware of an important tension between different ways of approaching Shakespeare. In his own lifetime, Shakespeare was entertainment, and commercial entertainment at that. He wrote the plays to be performed by professional acting companies who would stage the plays to audiences who paid to see them. He wrote for diverse audiences that might include educated nobility and illiterate peasants (the "groundlings") at the same show. That's why we often find crude slapstick humor mixed in with high-flown philosophy and poetry. Shakespeare tried to put something for everyone into his plays. In that sense his plays are analogous to modern film as popular and commercial entertainment. (Of course there are significant differences between small-scale theater in the Elizabethan era and big-budget Hollywood production and distribution systems in our own that would complicate, but not disqualify, this analogy.)

Somewhere between 1600 and English 399, Shakespeare was reinvented as "literature." A study of how this happened would be a book (if not an entire career) in itself. But as a student in a college Shakespeare course, you are participating in the ongoing production of Shakespeare as literature. You read the plays in a large and painstakingly edited anthology with footnotes and editorial apparatus that "frames" the plays as literary texts. You write papers, presumably, and get graded on your work. Eventually, you'll have credit for a Shakespeare course on your college transcript. Think about what that means for a moment. Shakespeare, probably more so than any other author in the English language, has come to signify a certain kind of education, a cultural privilege and value, all linked to the very interesting and problematic term "literature." Taking a course in Shakespeare has come to mean something in our culture, beyond the literal meaning that one has read and understood a certain number of the plays (and probably a few poems as well). It means one has access to certain (unnamed) cultural values, ideals, and aspirations.

As your English professors will tell you, the term "literature" can be understood in many different ways, and it has been contested and redefined since the 1960s by a range of new schools of thought, including feminist criticism, new historicism, performance theory, postcolonialism, and cultural studies, among others. Nonetheless, the term "literature" still does a certain kind of cultural work, and no discussion of Shakespeare can avoid engaging critically with the debate over the meaning and significance of literature or "the literary" as a cultural discourse.

So watching a Shakespeare film in the context of a college literature course provides an occasion for looking critically at the value of literature, its relationship to popular culture (and film), and the meaning of "Shakespeare" as what we might call a cultural icon. "Shakespeare" is both a myth (or icon) and an industry. He is a myth in the sense that readers and critics over the years have created a *persona* to attach to the name "William Shakespeare" in order to account for the existence of the plays and poems for which they have such great affection. (More accurately, there are in fact several different competing versions of this persona, depending on which critic or school you look at.) This persona has remarkably little to do with an actual person named William Shakespeare; it is primarily a creation based on interpretations of the texts. Nonetheless, people, including in this context filmmakers and directors, invest physical and emotional resources in this persona and create works of art informed by it. Shakespeare is also an industry—a critical industry, keeping many scholars, literary critics, and publishers busy; but also a broader cultural industry, involving tourism (in places like Stratford-on-Avon in England and Stratford in Ontario, Canada, among others), summer Shakespeare festivals, and of course films.

To some extent, any Shakespeare film necessarily engages "Shakespeare" as both a myth and an industry. The fact that it is identified as "a Shakespeare film" in the first place means that a whole range of expectations and ideals are going to be applied to such a film, whether consciously or not. A film can't *not* participate in the Shakespeare industry, nor can it avoid offering some kind of perspective on the myth of Shakespeare as author. As critical viewers, we can consider how a particular film participates in, resists, or even re-invents the myth of Shakespeare. Does the film present a "reverential" attitude toward the play and its author? Does it offer critical, playful, or even parodic views? Often a given film may do both, including moments of reverence alongside moments of campy parody. Rarely are films one-dimensional or without internal contradictions in their stance and approach to "Shakespeare."

9

There is a certain expectation for any film based on a Shakespeare play to stay "true" to the "original" (leaving aside the question of what that would be) and to capture and respect the depth and seriousness of the literary text. On the other hand, film is an entertainment medium, and filmmakers need to find ways to make the plays fun and accessible for viewers who have not studied the plays extensively or at all. These filmmakers can't assume, for example, that their audiences know the plots or that they have had experience listening to actors speaking in Shakespeare's early modern English. This tension, balancing between Shakespeare as high art and Shakespeare as popular entertainment, runs throughout the large body of cinematic work that has been produced over the past century.

The tension between entertainment and literature (or art) is one of the things that continues to make Shakespeare on film interesting and important. While some films may be more serious and literary, others more entertaining and playful, the point is that any particular film is going to be both things at the same time. Like any cultural text, it will be marked by internal contradictions. How we interpret and evaluate a film will depend on our framework of analysis and interpretation.

From Play to Film

Henry V, one of the history plays, opens with a speech by the Chorus that offers an important commentary on both the powers and the limitations of the stage. The language of this speech is worth looking at in detail, in part because it offers a somewhat unexpected perspective on the *limitations* rather than the powers of stage drama as a mode of representation. After we've looked at the passage itself, we'll turn to two contrasting film versions of this same scene. The first, from Laurence Olivier's 1944 film of *Henry V*, offers a plausible view of what a performance at The Globe theater in Shakespeare's own day might have looked like. We can explore some of the stage conventions Shakespeare would have used and think about the experience of watching one of the plays performed in its original historical context. The second, from

Kenneth Branagh's 1989 film adaptation, does for film what Olivier does for the stage. Branagh uses the opening Chorus to take us behind the scenes of modern filmmaking, offering a rich contrast to Olivier's historical representation of Elizabethan theater. Taken together, the two scenes can help us consider some of the major differences between the stage and the screen.

Here is the speech delivered by the Chorus at the opening of *Henry V*:

O, for a Muse of fire, that would ascend
The brightest heaven of invention!
A kingdom for a stage, princes to act,
And monarchs to behold the swelling scene!
Then should the warlike Harry, like himself,
Assume the port of Mars; and at his heels,
Leashed in like hounds, should famine, sword, and fire
Crouch for employment. But pardon, gentles all,
The flat unraisèd spirits that hath dared
On this unworthy scaffold to bring forth
So great an object. Can this cockpit hold
The vasty fields of France? Or may we cram
Within this wooden O the very casques
That did affright the air at Agincourt?
O, pardon! Since a crooked figure may
Attest in little place a million;
And let us, ciphers to this great account,
On your imaginary forces work.
Suppose within the girdle of these walls
Are now confined two mighty monarchies,
Whose high uprearèd and abutting fronts
The perilous narrow ocean parts asunder.
Piece out our imperfections with your thoughts:
Into a thousand parts divide one man,
And make imaginary puissance.
Think, when we talk of horses, that you see them
Printing their proud hoofs i' the receiving earth.
For 'tis your thoughts that now must deck our kings,

Carry them here and there, jumping o'er times,
Turning th' accomplishment of many years
Into an hourglass—for the which supply,
Admit me Chorus to this history,
Who, Prologue-like, your humble patience pray
Gently to hear, kindly to judge, our play. (Prologue, 1-34)

This passage combines two traditional ways of beginning a work. The first, the invocation of a muse, is a common convention in epic poetry: "O, for a Muse of fire." The muse being invoked here is warlike, epic, heroic, a muse "of fire." For only such a muse could help "warlike Harry [King Henry], like himself, / Assume the port of Mars"—only with a "kingdom for a stage" would there be enough room on stage to represent adequately the events of Henry's glorious victory over the French. The second tradition is the direct address to the audience. In this prologue, the Chorus serves as narrator, framing the story for the audience and asking for patience with the imperfections of the show. This narrator's address to the audience is a common device extending back to classical Athenian tragedy.

What's important here is the way the Chorus describes the limits of the stage. He says, in effect, that the events of this story are simply too big to be rendered effectively using the available resources in a little theater like The Globe. To his question, "Can this cockpit [the stage] hold / The vasty fields of France?" we implicitly answer, no, it can't—at least not literally. We recognize that no live stage performance can show us what the siege of Harfleur or the Battle of Agincourt really looked like. The "Muse of fire" would be able to show us the true face of war and the heroism of King Henry V at his moments of triumph; but alas, this Muse is nowhere to be found, and we are left instead with a crammed "wooden O" (The Globe theater itself, which was round) and the "unworthy scaffold" of the stage.

So the Chorus has to ask us to use our imaginations to transform a little theater into the battlefields of Agincourt, in order for the players to "dare" to present on stage the historical events of

King Henry's rise. As the audience for this spectacle, we are going to have to agree to play along, using our "imaginary forces" to transform one actor into "a thousand parts," "Turning th' accomplishment of many years / Into an hourglass" (the length of time it will take to watch the play).

Think about how this issue changes when we move from stage to screen. With the technology and the resources of modern filmmaking, it *is* in fact possible to recreate battles and sieges, to stage huge historical reenactments with hundreds of horses and thousands of soldiers, and to film the whole thing. Films like *Braveheart* or *Gladiator* clearly demonstrate the possibilities of recreating quite convincing images of medieval or classical warfare. Using a combination of live action and special effects, the technology of cinema can extend our field of vision into dimensions that an Elizabethan dramatist would not have been able to imagine. So what do you do with the Chorus and this opening scene if you're a director making a film instead of producing a live theatrical performance?

In his 1944 film, Laurence Olivier's answer was to film the opening prologue as a historical recreation of a live stage performance as it might have looked on May 1, 1600, in Shakespeare's own time. (This date appears on a poster shown as part of the opening credits of the film.) As Olivier's film opens, we see a wide shot looking out over an elaborate model of London in 1600. The actual model constructed for the film was, impressively, about 50 by 70 feet in size. The camera pulls back, moving out over the Thames from the Tower of London toward London Bridge before settling over two similar theater buildings along the near banks of the river. The camera teases us, hovering over the first theater-like building, which turns out to be the bear-bating arena, then descending into what we now recognize as The Globe, just as a flag is raised to signal the day's performance.

The scene shifts to the interior of the theater, and we watch the patrons milling about and settling into their seats. Vendors are hawking fruit and ale, and as the camera pans around the little arena, we glimpse a very realistic view of just what The Globe might have looked like moments before a performance of one of Shakespeare's plays. The audience is ranked in tiered seats around the perimeter, with the "groundlings" standing immediately at the foot of the stage. A few wealthy patrons are treated to stools on the edge of the stage itself.

An actor playing Shakespeare wearing thick reading glasses takes a stool at the far left edge of the stage, where he will serve as prompter for the actors. He then signals to the conductor to start the music. A young boy carrying a signboard comes out with a sign announcing the title of the play, and then the Chorus takes the stage to loud applause. Presumably the man is a well-known actor, and the audience greets his appearance on stage with a hearty welcome. About seven minutes into the film, we hear the first spoken words: "O, for a muse of fire...."

Olivier's directorial solution to the film *versus* drama issue is a clever one—his film is actually a film of a play or, rather, a play within a film. He chooses to make Shakespeare's play itself the subject of his film. What we are seeing here is not *Henry V*, the film, so much as *Henry V*, a film of the play as it looked in Shakespeare's day. The most interesting moment comes about two-thirds of the way through the opening prologue, however, when the illusion is itself broken. The actor (Leslie Banks) playing the Chorus actually steps toward the camera as it closes in on him, and he makes direct eye contact with the lens—it's as if he is breaking out of the frame of the play within the film to look directly at us, the audience of the film. This close-up happens just as he says "on your imaginary forces work," thereby making the same appeal to us that Shakespeare's Chorus makes to his live stage audience: Bear with us here, pretend, play along! Use your imagination and come with us on this great historical adventure!

As soon as this happens, the camera pulls back and the actor breaks eye contact, returning us to the feeling of watching from the upper balcony as the play takes place in 1600. There is only the one brief acknowledgment of our position as film spectators in this scene. At several points later in the film, Olivier will again play with the film *versus* stage distinction, moving back and forth between theatrical and cinematic modes of presentation.

Forty-five years later, in 1989, Kenneth Branagh remakes *Henry V* as his first feature Shakespeare film. How does Branagh handle the opening scene? Branagh's approach is to take us behind the scenes of the film itself. His film opens not in The Globe in 1600 but on a cluttered sound stage where *Henry V* is being filmed. The prologue begins in complete darkness. The Chorus (Derek Jacobi) strikes a single match to illuminate his face, beginning the speech: "O, for a muse of fire...." He walks down a small flight of steps, then flips a large circuit breaker to light up the scene, and we realize where we are: on a modern soundstage. The floor is littered with spotlights, a camera, candles, swords, banners, and other props. The back of the false walls read "HV." Throughout the opening prologue, Jacobi speaks directly to the camera—and, by extension, to us as his film audience. It's almost as if he is playing tour guide, taking us on a walking tour of the studio where Kenneth Branagh is hard at work on his new film, *Henry V*.

As Jacobi nears the end of the prologue, he moves toward a heavy set of medieval-looking doors. Just as he finishes his speech, "your humble patience pray / Gently to hear, kindly to judge, our play," he swings the doors open and the camera follows through into the darkness. We move with the camera from the frame of the prologue into the story space of the film itself, and the main action of the film begins. As the film continues, Branagh, like Olivier, plays back and forth along the boundaries of the film and its frame.

Because they both work so self-consciously with the distinctions between stage and screen, these two opening sequences prompt us to think about the relationship between film and drama as ways of representing the works of Shakespeare. The translation of Shakespeare's works happens on two levels when they are made into films. First, the works themselves must be imagined and visualized as dramatic productions. The plays have come down to us through history as texts, of course; stage

15

directions in Shakespeare are relatively sparse, presumably because Shakespeare himself was working directly with the actors and didn't need to write directions down since he was there at rehearsals. Thus the first translation happens when the text is transformed into a live drama. Any dramatic production is already an interpretation of the play itself.

A second translation follows when the drama is filmed: Now we have to make decisions about not only how to stage the play, but how to film it. Some of the films we will explore in more detail are relatively "straightforward" representations of the plays, produced more or less as retellings of the stories in a film environment. Others are more experimental or broader in their adaptations of the materials of the plays into film form. Richard Loncraine's *Richard III*, for example, moves the events of the play into a 1930s fascist environment, with a lead character (played by Ian McKellen) costumed to look suspiciously like Hitler. Julie Taymor's *Titus* takes *Titus Andronicus* (perhaps Shakespeare's bloodiest and most brutal play) into the world of postmodern spectacle, set in a strange theatrical universe that blends medieval costumes with motorcycles and backs it all with a punk-rock attitude.

But what Olivier's and Branagh's work with the opening prologues shows us is that the relationship between film and theater is complex and multidimensional. A film, as Olivier shows, can enclose within it a stage production. Just as Shakespeare often uses the device of the play within a play to dramatize things about the relationships between art and life, among other things, so too can film directors create a parallel device using the play within a film. As Branagh demonstrates, it's also possible to take Shakespeare's concept and adapt it, to create a film within a film. His *Henry V* repeatedly uses the devices of the chorus and the frame to look at the issue of historical representation and to pose questions about the nature of heroism, war, and epic for contemporary audiences.

Analysis and Interpretation: Henry V *opening sequence*

1. Watch the opening sequences of both versions of *Henry V* (Olivier's 1944 and Branagh's 1989 films are both available on DVD). Pay attention to the way each film takes viewers "backstage." How do these films represent the mechanics of stage and film production?

2. Many films try to make the relationship between the audience and the story as "seamless" as possible. Such films try to make us "forget" that we are watching a film that has been constructed to create the illusion of reality. In contrast, Shakespeare's drama often self-consciously reminds us that theater is an illusion or a game. So do these two films. Make a list of specific ways each of these opening sequences breaks the illusion to remind audiences that they are watching a film. How do these devices change your relationship to the story?

From Script to Screenplay

Like *Henry V*, *Romeo and Juliet* begins with a Chorus who serves as a narrator to the story, providing background information to help the audience understand what it will be watching. Here's how it begins:

> Two households both alike in dignity,
> In fair Verona where we lay our scene,
> From ancient grudge break to new mutiny,
> Where civil blood makes civil hands unclean.
> From forth the fatal loins of these two foes,
> A pair of star-crossed lovers take their life...

The Chorus tells us that this story is located in Verona, Italy; that two rival families of high standing have an ancient grudge that has once again broken out into new conflict and bloodshed; and that the children born to these two warring families are fated to be "star-crossed" in their love.

In a stage performance, it's quite likely that the Chorus would simply walk out to the front of the stage and deliver this

17

speech to the audience directly. Then he (or she) would step aside or pull back a curtain to begin the play's opening fight sequence. How might this be handled in a film? Baz Luhrmann's clever solution in his 1996 film, *William Shakespeare's Romeo + Juliet*, is to transform the Chorus into a television news anchor. Luhrmann intersperses segments of the anchor's speech with segments from the opening fight scene, moving back and forth between external shots of the fight scene (Act 1, Scene 1), set in a gas station parking lot, and her choral prelude, delivered from an interior television studio. (This back-and-forth editing movement is called *intercutting*.) Here is the opening sequence, as it appears in the screenplay by Craig Pearce and Baz Luhrmann:

EXT. HIGHWAY. AFTERNOON.
A ribbon of freeway stretching into a blue and pink late afternoon sky. A huge dark sedan, windows tinted gold, powers directly for us.
CUT TO: A heavy, low slung pickup truck traveling toward the sedan.
WIDE SHOT: Sky, freeway, the cars closing.
TIGHT ON: The sedan.
TIGHT ON: The pickup.
Like thunderous, jousting opponents, the cars pass in a deafening cacophony of noise.

INT. TRUCK. AFTERNOON.
TIGHT ON: The fat face of GREGORY, yelling at the disappearing sedan.

          GREGORY
A dog of the house of Capulet moves me!

He and the pimply-faced front-seat passenger, SAMPSON, explode with laughter.
The red-haired driver, BENVOLIO, keeps his eyes on the road.

INT. TV STUDIO. DAY.

An ANCHORWOMAN; behind the faces of two middle-aged men. The caption reads, "Montague; Capulet. The feud continues."

She speaks to the camera.

ANCHORWOMAN

Two households both alike in dignity.
(In fair Verona, where we lay our scene)
From ancient grudge break to new mutiny,
Where civil blood makes civil hands unclean.

EXT. GAS STATION. AFTERNOON.
The truck is in the busy driveway of a large gas station, being filled with gas. The surrounding walls are painted with murals of blue sky and palm trees. (pp. 1-2)

Most of what we read here is actually visual description of each scene or shot (camera position), as visualized by the director. (INT is an abbreviation for interior, EXT for exterior, indicating the location of each sequence, whether indoors or outside.) The position of the camera is recorded for each scene: Cuts, wide shots, and tight shots are described for each segment of the film. (A cut represents an edit that shifts to a new camera location; a wide shot is filmed with the camera at a distance, using a wide-angle lens, so that the camera takes in a large background behind the subject; a tight shot, in contrast, pulls the camera in close to the subject and narrows the field of view.) In all, only five lines from the play itself appear here (Gregory's taunt to the passing Capulet car, and the first four lines of the Chorus). The rest of the space is taken up with specific description of the scene as visualized by the director and screenwriter.

Luhrmann creates a sense of visual tension and drama by cutting quickly back and forth between the fight scene at the gas station and the news anchor's report of the renewed violence. The rest of the lines of the Chorus are spoken as voice-overs several pages later. (In a voice-over, we hear an actor speaking, offscreen, while we watch something else happen. Voice-overs are often used to signify narrators telling a story in flashback or remembering something that has happened earlier.) In Luhrmann's version, the events play out on the screen simultaneously with the narrator's framing for the audience.

Even this brief excerpt from a screenplay suggests how much work goes into transforming the text of a Shakespeare play into a screenplay for a film. Screenwriters and directors have to think about each scene and each shot within that scene: where to set it, what the actors look like, where the camera is positioned, how and when the lines are delivered, and so forth. Usually, a screenplay will serve as the basis for a set of storyboards, visual sketches (looking rather like a comic book) that represent each shot or sequence in the film. From such storyboards, an even more detailed shooting script is developed before filming can begin.

If you've studied film before, or worked on a film yourself, you understand the labor-intensive process that is required to go from a story (or play, or idea, or concept sketch) to a complete film. And filming itself is only part of the process; after filming is complete, editing and post-production crews go to work, molding hours and hours of film footage into a carefully sequenced series of scenes that will work for audiences and adding sound, music, effects, and so forth.

It can be quite useful, particularly if you are writing an essay on a film (or films), to have a copy of the screenplay or to create one of your own. You can create your own "scene outline" for specific sequences to describe the way each scene is setup and filmed (as we will do later in this chapter). This strategy can help to understand the complex structuring process used to transform the text/script of a play into a dynamic visual medium.

Experiencing Drama and Film

Let's take a step back at this point and consider some of the differences between attending a live theatrical performance and watching a film. A live theatrical performance is an immediate, living event. We are physically present in a time and place with the actors who are speaking and dancing and moving about the stage in a choreography of bodies. Their presence and their direct interaction with the audience lend a dynamic interchange to the event. Fed by the audience's laughter, it is often the clowns and the comic characters that steal the show. The comedies, especially, come to life on stage in a way that can be hard to replicate on film (let alone on the page). The verbal humor, puns, and physical comedy can be very hard to get from the text of the play in silent reading, but in live drama the action and life can be breathed back into the play in surprising and delightful ways.

Because of the large space of the theater, the actors have to project their voices in a live performance. We become accustomed to exaggerated voices and gestures; even asides and whispers must sometimes be shouted out, especially in the large outdoor theaters where summer Shakespeare festivals are frequently presented. For soliloquies, the convention is usually for the actor to step toward the edge of the stage and to directly address the audience. Even though he is projecting a loud stage voice, we understand and accept that Hamlet, for example, is "thinking to himself" as he wonders whether or not to be. Just as there is no equivalent of a close-up shot in a live performance, there's also no voice-over or dramatic interior monologue—we simply accept that the soliloquy represents such an inner debate or conversation.

In a theater, our point of view is generally fixed. Unless we switch seats or watch from backstage, we are more or less stuck in place as we watch the show from our seats. The space of the stage is a bounded space, and we view it from a single, stationary point of view. While we have the freedom to focus on whatever we like, we generally do so within a fairly defined frame of vision. Within this visual space, the movement of the actors' bodies can itself make a kind of choreographed effect. Characters can huddle together at the center of the stage; they can run off in separate directions as an alarm sounds. Their spatial relationships can be used to create dramatic tension: One actor may be looming over another or up in a balcony; actors may be positioned on the stage to suggest conflict (through distance or visual hierarchy); they can move toward or away from one another; and so forth. But throughout these visual movements, our perspective is more or less fixed in place and it is the actors and sometimes the sets that move.

In the cinema, our point of view moves with the camera. We can move in very close, to overhear whispered confidences between two actors, or we can pull way back to see an entire battlefield from miles off in the distance. We can roll around a scene (as when the camera is mounted on a "dolly" or rolling track), our viewpoint moving dynamically to see events unfold from a changing perspective. However it is handled in a particular film, the camera *mediates* our relationship to the actors in a film, inserting a crucial distance between us and the performers that is not present in live drama. Some directors use relatively fixed cameras to create a viewing experience that is more like watching a play; others may move wildly about the space of the film with a highly dynamic camera, creating effects and experiences that are radically cinematic and impossible in a live play.

Sound and audio effects can also work quite differently in a film. Soliloquies can be done as "voice-overs," where a character is heard speaking but is not necessarily talking out loud or addressing us directly. The convention of the filmic voice-over is so familiar to us that we assume an off-screen voice is "thinking" rather than talking. Filmmakers can use this to great advantage when adapting some of the major scenes and speeches to the screen. Combined with the mobile camera, the use of audio and voice-over can enhance our experience of the psychological overtones of some of Shakespeare's writing. A voice-over can be combined with visual imagery so as to place us, metaphorically, inside the characters' minds. Film can be used to amplify such interior monologues in a way that can be hinted at but not directly represented in a live performance.

In place of live theater's immediacy, film offers us an edited construction. The director has tighter control over our attention (we see what the camera shows us) and can also use editing techniques and other devices to construct an experience for us. In watching a film, at least in the context of home video and DVD, we can always pause, rewind, or fast forward, and thus re-experience the film in ways its director could not have intended.

The common element linking the films we'll explore with live performances is above all the language. With very few exceptions, the films we'll discuss in *Screening Shakespeare* stick to Shakespeare's scripted language and do not attempt to translate Elizabethan idioms into contemporary speech. Many of the films use excerpted and edited versions of the play scripts, of course. One notable exception is Kenneth Branagh's *Hamlet*, which does use the complete text of the play (with a few minor edits), and which runs four hours long as a result. The scenes and the historical contexts may be changed, sometimes radically, in some of the films, but the lines being spoken by the actors are still those that were written by Shakespeare.

Beyond the language, the stories themselves are usually the same and survive the translation into film. Hamlet still despises his stepfather and worries about his mother. Lear's daughters still fight over the inheritance. These stories may be plotted and represented differently in film, but they are still in some meaningful sense the same stories. Rather than speak of live performance and film as completely distinct, separate categories, we'll view them here in a more complex relationship, as we've seen in the example of the prologue to *Henry V*. Instead of an absolute divide between theater and film, many of the examples we'll discuss in these pages play on the fact that there is a continuum between live drama on one end and mediated cinema on the other. As critical viewers and informed readers of the plays, we can learn much from the interaction of dramatic and cinematic elements in the major films.

Inquiries: The Experience of Viewing

1. Make a list of key differences between attending a live stage performance and watching a film. If you've recently attended a Shakespeare performance, try to capture as many details as you can remember. How is your involvement in a play different from your experience of a film? How does the experience of

film change as you move from the large screen of the cineplex to the small screen of home video?

2. Shakespeare plays often have speeches (soliloquies) designed to represent a character's inner thoughts. How have you seen this handled on the stage? What different techniques have you seen in films to represent a character's thoughts?

3. Can you think of specific plays or types of plays that would be better in live theater than on film? What are the advantages of live drama for each genre (comedy, tragedy, history, or romance)?

Three Approaches to Studying Shakespeare Films

Whether we're watching a film for enjoyment or for scholarly purposes, we're always using some kind of framework or theory. Even the idea of watching a film for "mindless entertainment" is itself a crude kind of film theory. When we turn to films based on Shakespeare's plays, our first point of reference is most likely going to come from our prior experiences with Shakespeare. Our experience of a film will be different if we know a play well, in contrast to watching a film of a play we've never read. In my own case, I knew the play *Hamlet* well and had seen four other films of the play prior to my first experience watching Michael Almereyda's film (featuring Ethan Hawke as Hamlet). I could in a sense only "read" that film in the context of my own history with the play. This meant that I tended to interpret Almereyda's film as a commentary on the previous films and also as an attempt to produce a distinctly "contemporary" or even "postmodern" version of the play. In contrast, I was not very familiar with *Titus Andronicus* the first time I watched Julie Taymor's *Titus*, so I found myself asking a different set of questions about the play and Taymor's interpretation of it. I was less sure about what Taymor had created and what came from the Shakespeare play.

Film as literary adaptation

We're analyzing films in the context of a Shakespeare course rather than, say, a film history course, and therefore our first framework or point of reference will be the texts of Shakespeare's plays. In a film history course, we might choose to look at Laurence Olivier's *Hamlet* (1948) in the context of other psychological thrillers of that time period (which popularized a style known as *film noir*). Instead, our focus will be on Olivier's *Hamlet* in comparison to other filmed *Hamlets*.

The literary context provides our first framework for analyzing the films. A framework or a theory is, above all, a way of posing certain kinds of questions. Literary and film theory can help substantiate our approaches to films here by framing certain types of inquiry. Our first line of inquiry centers around the questions related to how each film offers an interpretation of the text of a given play.

Think about the kinds of decisions directors like Olivier and Branagh had to make in composing scenes like the prologue to *Henry V* that we looked at earlier. Initial questions might have been whether to film the prologue at all and whether or not to include the Chorus as a character in the film. Since the purpose of the prologue is to ask the audience to use its imagination to transform the stage into an epic battlefield, it might be irrelevant if the film actually shows the battles (as both of these do) and the audience for the film would be able to see those things the original spectators wouldn't have. It's quite possible either director could have edited the prologue out and moved directly into the action of the play, beginning with the debate over the legitimacy of Henry's claim to France. Why didn't they do it that way? Why did both Olivier and Branagh decide to keep the figure of the Chorus, begin with the prologue, and "frame" their films using the dramatic device of the Chorus and his direct address to the audience?

Questions like these can be discovered in almost every moment of a Shakespeare film. Screenplays rarely follow the text of the play exactly—characters may be edited out, combined, or revised in some way. Entire scenes may not be included. In the case of *Henry V*, both Olivier and Branagh include brief "flashbacks" to Henry's earlier friendship with Falstaff, using lines that actually come from *2 Henry IV*, the previous play in the historical sequence.

The first time you watch a film, it may be best to sit back and watch to get a feel for how the film works. Such a first viewing is often called a "participatory" reading, a process that can be applied to reading a literary text on the page as well as viewing a film. On a second viewing, however, it's helpful to follow along with the text, marking the lines that are included and getting a sense for the outline of the script. You will notice patterns in how the play's text is edited, shaped, and crafted for presentation onscreen. This type of reading is often called an "analytical" reading, to indicate that you are moving from participation to analysis, breaking a film down into its components for closer study.

One useful practice in analytical reading is to develop a scene outline, where you make note of each scene in the film and its corresponding lines in the play. Here's an excerpt from a scene outline I created for Michael Almereyda's *Hamlet*.

1. [0:00] Open on a view of NYC towers through the back window of a limousine. Legend reads: "New York City, 2000 / The King and C.E.O of Denmark Corporation is Dead / The King's widow has hastily remarried his younger brother / The King's son, Hamlet, returns from school, suspecting foul play . . ."

2. (2.2) [0:52] Times Square: Hamlet walks across the street to his room at Hotel Elsinore. In his room, recorded on his personal video player, we see grainy B&W images of Hamlet himself, speaking: "I have of late...lost all my mirth..../ What a piece of work is a man..." (from 2.2) His phone rings. On the screen, images of animal skeletons, the Gulf War, and a B-2 bomber taking off. "And yet to me what is this quintessence of dust?"

3. [2:35] Title screen (blood-red background)

Each numbered section corresponds to one scene or continuous sequence in the film. Usually there are clear breaks between scenes (fades to black, dissolves, or some other film notation to signal a shift in time or place), but sometimes you simply make arbitrary decisions to break a sequence of shots into a numbered scene. There's no "right" way to do this; the purpose of a scene outline is to help you get a sense for the shape and structure of the film. Use whatever method makes sense to you for a given film. Here we have outlined the first three scenes, making up a total of about three minutes of screen time.

The numbers in the square brackets refer to the time of the film, beginning at 0:00 and running sequentially through each scene. (You can get this number from your VCR or DVD player quite easily. It helps to track how much screen time is devoted to each scene.) The numbers in parentheses represent the corresponding act and scene numbers from Shakespeare's play. In this case, it's interesting to note that Almereyda presents parts of Act 2, Scene 2 (2.2) *before* Act 1, Scene 2.

For each scene, provide a brief description of what is presented on the screen, paying attention to how each image is framed and composed as well as who is doing and saying what. Breaking down a film and annotating it in order to create a scene outline like this helps to understand how a particular film adapts the text of the play. It also helps to see the extent to which the film is a constructed, formal artifact, a carefully and artfully produced assemblage of individual shots. Remember that any performance, dramatic or cinematic, necessarily has to make certain interpretive decisions about the play.

Influenced (perhaps unconsciously) by Shakespeare's status as cultural icon, many reviewers and critics approach films based on his plays in terms of how well or how "authentically" they represent the "original" play. In such an approach, Laurence Olivier might be criticized (as in fact he was) for adding a voice-over at the beginning of *Hamlet* or for not including the Fortinbras subplot. As interesting and helpful as it can be to compare a film with the literary text it is based on, it's important to resist the impulse to fall into the assumption that Shakespeare's text represents some ideal that a given film has to live up to. In a sense, *adaptation* is not exactly the right word to use here, because any film is itself a performance or reinvention of the play and is more constructive of meaning than the rather passive term *adaptation* might suggest.

This is especially true in the case of Shakespeare. As you probably know, no true "original" text exists for any of Shakespeare's plays. The scripts that you read in your textbooks are edited reconstructions based on historical and textual scholarship, and the location of lines, the spelling and meaning of words, the stage directions, and many other details continue to be the subject of intense debate. Even an edition of a Shakespeare play is itself already a kind of performance. We simply do not know exactly "what Shakespeare meant to say."

Consider that a filmmaker may be working from a different edition of the text, and that he or she may hold a very different interpretation of the play than what you are familiar with. The meaning that is created in and by a Shakespeare film is perhaps best seen as a dialogue with the text of the play (rather than an adaptation). A film in a sense "talks back" to the play, placing it in a new and different context, reworking its language to produce what is often a very different and even unexpected meaning.

Film as a formal work

As you begin to analyze the ways a film works with the text of a play to shape and present it for the screen, you come to recognize the importance of film form and strategy in the creation of a cinematic experience for viewers. The study of film as an art form is a discipline in its own right, and if you have never taken a film course or studied film in an academic setting, some of the terms and concepts may be new to you. We'll try to define them and use specific examples wherever possible. A great resource for students and film enthusiasts is *Film Art: An Introduction*, by David Bordwell and Kristin Thompson (6th ed., 2001), a book that is widely used as a text for undergraduate film courses. We'll refer to that book as a resource often, especially for its definitions and illustrations of formal techniques in film.

The opening sequence of a film is especially important; it introduces viewers to the world of the film and it guides us into the space of the film and its story, setting up certain expectations about where we are and what that place is like. In the example of the two *Henry V* films we looked at earlier, we can see two different strategies at work. The Olivier film announces itself as a historical recreation almost immediately, from the choice of type font used in the credits to the elaborate model of London that is the first visual image presented onscreen. The opening sequence is framed as a film about a play being performed live at The Globe Playhouse in 1600.

We are situated by the film as a member of the live audience seated in the upper tiers of the house. By the time the Chorus takes the stage to speak the opening lines, we already understand that we are watching a play within a film. We expect certain things as a result, and then the film can play with those expectations to create a sense of drama and surprise. So when, for example, Leslie Banks moves toward the camera for a close-up, looks directly "at us," and says "on your imaginary forces work," we feel we are being directly addressed—at the same time we are reminded that we are experiencing a film and not a play. Olivier continues to make use of this surprise, as his scene eventually does shift away from the reconstructed Globe to Southampton, and on to the fields of France.

The Branagh film self-consciously places us squarely in the middle of the world of filmmaking. As Derek Jacobi wanders through the sets and props, we are reminded that films are not magic; they are crafted and acted and edited and built by people through a very labor-intensive, collaborative process. Branagh's opening sequence echoes Olivier's in its use of the prologue, but for Branagh it is important to frame the tale not in terms of the stage but in terms of the craft of film. We see Jacobi standing there with a camera in the foreground and we cannot help but remember that film, like theater, is an illusion—a game in which we willingly participate.

The world created for us by the opening of a film creates expectations that the film may later use, subvert, or modify in some way, but those first few moments establish the vital relationship between the viewer and the film. Once we have entered into the story-world of a film, we can study it for its production design. What kind of a world has this film presented to us? *Hamlet*, for example, has been filmed in several very different kinds of settings: in a dark, foggy medieval castle, isolated from the world; in an 18th-century country house, a world of spectacle and lavish beauty; and in contemporary Manhattan, where the characters carry laptops but speak Elizabethan English. Set design, location, and *mise-en-scene* all work together in a film to create this fictional cinematic world.

Mise-en-scene is a French term that literally means "putting into the scene," and it includes all of the visual elements that contribute to what viewers see. Bordwell and Thompson include setting, costume, make-up, lighting, staging, and acting under the umbrella of *mise-en-scene*. Others define *mise-en-scene* somewhat more narrowly, using the term to emphasize details and objects that appear in a shot or in the background to create a theme or an atmosphere.

A film may establish a surreal, mystical landscape (like Kurosawa's version of Macbeth, *Throne of Blood*) or it may create a very "realistic" landscape such as contemporary New York City. The visual creation of this film world is a crucial part of the language of a given film, and it is to the filmed story what set design and costuming is to live theater. In both cases, the visual elements of the setting help to create a specific environment that works on us on a literal and an emotional level.

In approaching film on a formal level, we also pay attention to the camera: How is it positioned? Is it moving or static? The camera serves as the audience's eyes in a film, and it's important to pay attention to where the director and the cinematographer are guiding our gaze. There are many different types of camera angles and movements, and we'll define and discuss most of them in context as they arise. We'll also often want to attend closely to the role of the camera in creating the film as we experience it.

Notice, for example, the importance of the camera's movement in the opening of Olivier's *Henry V*: It begins with a very wide shot of the cityscape of London, takes us on a visual "tour" of the city in 1600 before closing in and descending down from a high vantage point (an aerial view) into the space of The Globe itself. We enter the world of the theater from a great distance, and the effect is to create a sweeping, epic context for the opening moments of the film. In contrast, Branagh's camera begins with a very tight shot of Jacobi's face lit by a single match. The effect is more claustrophobic—we begin in total darkness. Then the camera's gaze follows the Chorus through the crowded and cluttered sets backstage before exploding visually into the world of the film itself. We move with the camera through a set of heavy doors into the space of the film's story, and the overall effect is more dark, enclosed, foreboding than that of Olivier's opening.

An additional layer of formal analysis comes from a study of the way a film is edited. Editing works closely with the camera to create the visual feel of a film. The editing establishes a rhythm and pacing for the film: Are there lots of long takes, or many short shots spliced rapidly together? Is the scene interrupted by many edits and new camera angles, or do we stay with a particular shot or vantage point for an extended time? A filmmaker like Baz Luhrmann tends to use rapid-fire editing to create a breathless, visually chaotic, and startling effect for viewers. Laurence Olivier generally employs a slower pacing, an effect that tends to draw us more deeply into the psychological subtexts of brooding characters like Hamlet.

Sound and music provide an additional layer of film form that we'll want to pay attention to as we look at specific films. Music creates a mood in a film, and recurring songs or themes can serve to develop sound links or sound bridges from one scene to another or to echo back to an earlier moment in a film. Sound effects and other audio used in a film also create formal meaning in specific ways. Almereyda's *Hamlet*, for example, uses video and digital footage within the film to create a voice-over narration for some of Hamlet's speeches. Rather than hearing Hamlet speaking directly, we hear his grainy, recorded voice instead. The film poses important questions through that use of sound about the way human relationships are now mediated by technology.

Like the beginning sequence of a film, the ending also carries special weight. As you analyze a film for its construction as a formal work, pay attention to the way it ends. Closing images often leave the most powerful and lasting impression on an audience.

Film as cultural text

When we analyze a film as literary adaptation, we look for its meaning primarily in relation to the literary texts and traditions it engages. In our second framework, we shift to a new context, considering how a film uses the conventions, forms, codes, and devices of cinema art to produce meaning as a formal construct in the context of other films. Our third interpretive strategy or framework shifts to yet a third context. Here, we look at film in the broader context of culture. What, in this context, do we mean by culture? How does this view shape our understanding of films?

The meaning of the word *culture* has shifted and expanded over the last few decades, as scholars in several disciplines, including women's studies, history, anthropology, semiotics, media studies, and literature, have worked to challenge the notion of culture as exclusively the domain of "high art" and class prestige. In a sense, this new understanding shifts the definition of *culture* from something one *has* (or does not have) to something one *does*. If you think of culture in the narrower, traditional sense of the word, you are likely to imagine things like ballet, opera, and maybe even Shakespeare. People who are "cultured" participate in these events and gain access to certain kinds of power and prestige as a result. Our newer definition of culture, however, is not restricted to this class-specific understanding. Instead, we now tend to define culture as a way of life: a process we use to negotiate our way through everyday life, make sense of what's happening, and assign meaning and value to a wide range of texts, events, and things.

Culture is a system of codes and strategies that we use to make meaning in a nearly infinite number of ways. We can only begin to understand and make sense of events and daily life when we have a context or framework to relate them to, and in this sense, culture is that which provides these frameworks for understanding who we are and what we're doing. For example, think about your own experience as a college student. That experience is mediated through a whole host of cultural codes of different types. The way you understand and experience the identity of "college student" is a result of your use of and interaction with these codes. One code is college as an "ivory tower," a place one goes to get away from the immediate and practical demands of life to think and study. Sometimes this implies, subtly or not, that college is a waste of time, impractical, and detached from the real things that matter. Many college professors are viewed by students as aloof, detached, or out of touch, a symptom of the power and persistence of the code of college as ivory tower. A different cultural code suggests college as youthful celebration, a place for frat parties and late-night revelry. (A whole book could be written about the films that rework this cultural tradition, from *Animal House* to *Old School*.) A third code signifies college as a route to a better career and a better life. We might call this the code of college as upward mobility. All of these cultural codes, and many others, structure and filter your experience of "college life" on a daily basis.

Exploring the cultural discourses linked to the identity of "college student" might not provide much insight into a Shakespeare film. But there are other cultural codes that undoubtedly do produce significant results. Take, for example, the issues of gender and sexuality. Feminist literary critics were among the earliest readers of Shakespeare to demonstrate how the plays reproduced the cultural assumptions about men and women and the relationships between them that were typical of Elizabethan England. By shifting the analysis from Shakespeare as literature to Shakespeare as a cultural text, feminist scholars were able to demonstrate the complex relationships between Shakespeare's representations of gender and other non-literary representations of gender in legal codes, property ownership, popular culture, and so forth.

We can make a similar interpretive move with the films. By looking at the representations of women and men, femininity and masculinity, we can explore how these films both participate in and (sometimes) critique or disrupt the dominant codes and discourses of modern patriarchy. This is usually a complex matter—rarely is a specific film either purely "sexist" or purely "feminist" in its representations of gender and power. It is almost always the case that a mainstream feature film will to some extent reproduce the dominant codes and ideologies of its times. In order to appeal to an audience large enough to support the costs of making a feature film, filmmakers need to produce films that "make sense" to their audiences—meaning that they tend to reproduce some or most of the dominant culture's expectations and values. This may not always be true of small-budget or art-house films, which aim to be aesthetically and culturally disruptive (Derek Jarman's *The Tempest*, for example, foregrounds homoeroticism in ways that might offend some mainstream film audiences.) Most films offer moments where they subvert (or potentially subvert) dominant representations of gender and power, just as they have moments that reproduce those dominant codes. The point is to explore the contradictions and complexities.

Like feminist literary criticism, feminist film theory has developed into a discipline in its own right over the past three decades or so. Feminist film theory started out by looking at the way women were represented in film. Did film offer positive images of strong women? Did film offer women alternative ways to experience femininity and female sexuality outside of the domain of patriarchy and consumer culture? From there, feminist film theory has evolved in several directions. Feminist theorists explore the power of "the gaze": Who is looking? Who is being looked at? How does a film position its viewers as spectators? Are we assumed to take a "male" position as we watch? What would a female or femimist viewpoint "look like" in film? Feminist film theory draws extensively on Freudian and post-Freudian theories of sexuality, theories of spectatorship and subjectivity developed from French poststructuralism, as well as the productive work of feminist filmmakers and screenwriters around the world. It's a rich and complex field, and my description doesn't even scratch the surface. There's a great deal of work to be done in Shakespeare film studies by scholars and students who want to apply a feminist lens to the filmmakers' works.

Gender differences are not the only issues that come to the forefront when we look at films as cultural texts. Culture is where meaning and power intersect, and just as gender is one specific node in the matrix of power and discourse, so too are race, social class, sexuality, and ethnicity parts of a field of cultural and linguistic difference. Some of Shakespeare's plays address issues of racial and ethnic difference explicity; *Othello* and *The Merchant of Venice* come to mind as plays in which race and ethnicity figure as principal elements of the plot. But even plays and films that do not at first appear to be "about" race or ethnicity can be interpreted and analyzed for their representations of such differences (or their apparent silence on the subjects). Social class figures prominently in many of the plays and can be a subject for analysis as well. The point in analyzing film from a cultural perspective is to look beyond the surface to consider how the language, imagery, and formal elements of the film construct relationships of power and meaning at virtually every moment.

Shakespeare, as we discussed earlier, remains a powerful cultural force, as a highly "literary" author and as a cultural myth or icon. In taking a cultural approach to Shakespeare films, we are less concerned with how adequately those films represent the plays and more interested in considering how they can be "read" (viewed critically) and interpreted in the context of contemporary culture. Shakespeare films circulate and compete in a densely populated cultural landscape. To a certain extent, they are part of popular culture as much as literary culture or literary history. As you watch a film like Baz Luhrmann's *Romeo + Juliet*, you might want to think about how it compares to other "love stories" you have seen on film. What kind of meaning can you discover in the way Luhrmann's film plays with conventions of teenage love and romance? What about the religious symbolism? How do Catholic and Latino cultural references add to the layers of meaning? How does it change your understanding of Tybalt to see his character played by John Leguizamo? Questions like these, and many others, can be generated when we approach films as cultural texts. There is no limit to the ways Shakespeare films can be reinterpreted when you place them in the context of contemporary culture.

Checklist of Working Questions for Analyzing Films

This checklist is intended to suggest some of the lines of inquiry you might take when adopting each of the three frameworks or interpretive strategies discussed in this chapter. These questions are meant to be suggestive rather than exhaustive. Use them to generate your own questions, and return to this list as you consider specific films, to add questions, modify or adapt them, and develop more refined approaches.

Film as literary adaptation

✓ How much of the play's text is used in the film? How is the text of the play edited, cut, reorganized, or rewritten within the film? Which version of the text is the screenplay based on?

✓ Which characters does the film focus on? Are certain characters given more (or less) emphasis in the film than in the play?

✓ How are key scenes and speeches in the play presented in the film? Does the film seem to offer any specific interpretations of the meanings or motivations of the characters' actions and words?

✓ How is the language of the play supported by the acting, visual elements, and editing of the film?

Film as a formal work

✓ How does the film begin? How are viewers introduced to the story world of the film? Where are we positioned or situated as spectators? What expectations are established in the opening sequence?

✓ How do the location, set design, costuming, and other elements of *mise-en-scene* create a fictional world? How would you describe the visual setting or environment? What effect does it have on the mood and tone of the film?

✓ How is the camera used? Is it mobile, static? Does the camera stay close in or move back to a distance?

✓ How does the editing create rhythm and continuity in the film? Is the pacing slow or fast? Are editing techniques used to create tension or contrast?

✓ How does the film end? Where are viewers left at the close of the film? Are we given any retrospective distance on the story? Is the narrative framed? Does the ending offer a sense of closure?

Film as cultural text

✓ When was the film made? What social and historical contexts does it seem to be responding to, explicitly or implicitly? What about the film seems dated? Why? What seems current or contemporary?

✓ How does the film reinterpret the themes of the original play into a contemporary context or setting?

✓ How are relationships between men and women represented? Does the film rely on conventional definitions of masculinity and femininity? Does it offer any contrasting or unconventional representations of gender and gender difference? What kind of power do men possess and use? What kind of power do women possess and use?

✓ Are there any nonhuman characters in the film (witches, fairies, mythical creatures, gods and goddesses, ghosts)? How are these characters represented? How do they interact with human characters? What kind of language and imagery is used to describe them? Do these nonhuman characters seem to have a gender? A racial or ethnic identity? What function do these characters serve in the film?

✓ Does the film present any religious or cultural images or icons (crosses, cathedrals, cemeteries, temples, or masks)? How are their meanings used in the film? What do they signify? How are their meanings changed or influenced by the events of the story?

✓ Which characters in the film are marked or identified by their social class or economic status? Are any characters unmarked by class difference? Does social class have any relationship to power in the film? Do any characters move from one class to another? How?

✓ Does the film echo or allude to other cultural texts (other Shakespeare texts, other literary texts generally, other films, popular culture, or music)? How are these "intertexts" significant in the film?

Questions for Writing and Discussion

1. Create your own list of differences between film and live drama. Think back on plays and films you've attended and how those experiences affected you as a viewer. What strikes you about the nature of the two different forms? In what ways are film and drama similar? Do they create similar feelings and

responses in their audiences? What social or cultural purposes does each serve?

2. Take a favorite scene from one of the plays you have been reading recently and look at it through the eyes of a film director. Think about how you would film the scene for a movie you are working on. What kinds of decisions would you have to make? How would you approach the scene differently if you were producing it for live performance?

3. Watch the opening sequence of a film version of one of the plays you are currently reading in class (consult the filmography in the back of this book to help identify relevant films available on DVD or VHS). Make note of as many cinema-specific moments as you can: Are there places where the camera moves? Close-up shots? Voice-overs? Create a list of the techniques and devices used in the film that would not be possible in a live performance.

4. Take one of the plays you are reading and imagine you are the casting director for a new film to be made based on this play. Who would you choose to play each of the roles? Why? How did you make your choices? What criteria did you use in selecting them? How would your film be different with a different cast?

CHAPTER 2

The Comedies

It's a common joke that all of Shakespeare's comedies end with weddings and all his tragedies with funerals. While this may not be literally true, it is indeed the case that many of the comedies end on a note of celebratory closure, marked by a wedding or festival. No matter how complicated the conflicts may have gotten during the main action of the play, the ending will generally be marked by a sense of resolution and the return of order. Some of these resolutions may strike modern audiences as contrived or unrealistic—too many things have to fall into place for characters to get out of their self-imposed messy situations—but nonetheless the movement of the comic plots almost always tends toward the reassertion of order and stability. Of all the major genres Shakespeare wrote in, comedy is the most formulaic.

Comic Form and Structure

It's often quite useful, when coming to terms with one of the comedies for the first time, to divide its story into three parts. The first part is the initial state or order of the fictional world. In the second part, this order is disrupted by some force, dilemma, person, or conflict. The third part is usually marked by the return of order and the resolution of the conflict or disruption. Some of Shakespeare's later "problem" comedies do not fit this model, but most of the early and middle period comedies do. This is a somewhat crude and schematic way to view the plots, but it can be a useful starting point for analyzing filmed versions of the comedies.

Literary critic Northrop Frye describes comedy as "the mythos of spring" and outlines comic structure as follows.

What normally happens is that a young man wants a young woman, that his desire is resisted by some opposition, usually paternal, and that near the end of the play some twist in the plot enables the hero to have his will. In this simple pattern there are several complex elements. In the first place, the movement of comedy is usually a movement from one kind of society to another. At the beginning of the play, the obstructing characters are in charge of the play's society, and the audience recognizes that they are usurpers. At the end of the play the device in the plot that brings the hero and heroine together causes a new society to crystallize around the hero.... The appearance of this new society is frequently signalized by some kind of party or festive ritual, which either appears at the end of the play or is assumed to take place immediately afterward. (*Anatomy of Criticism*, 163)

Frye's theories have been criticized for several reasons. Feminists have argued that his model privileges male heroes and ignores the specificity of gender differences in many of the works he analyzes. Historicist critics have demonstrated that his archetypes are ahistorical and do not allow for social context or patterns of change or evolution over time in the literary genres. So I'm not suggesting that we adopt Frye as an overarching framework for the analysis of Shakespeare films. What I would argue, however, is that Frye's model of comic structure can help us begin to see some of the larger elements and plot dynamics that operate in some of the comedies on film.

In *A Midsummer Night's Dream*, for example, the initial order or society is the world of the Athenian court and its laws and authority. This authority is represented in the figures of Theseus, the Duke of Athens, and Egeus, a member of the nobility (ruling class) and father to Hermia. Egeus's authority is challenged by his daughter, Hermia, who resists the arranged marriage preferred by her father and wants instead to marry Lysander, to whom she is emotionally and romantically attached. Theseus attempts to intervene on behalf of Egeus and the patriarchal authority he represents by invoking a law that says Hermia must accept her father's choice of a husband or be punished by death. So our initial order is represented by Theseus and Egeus, who stand for patriarchal authority and established rules. The complication or disruption that challenges this order is romantic love and desire, identified with Hermia and Lysander.

In order to escape the laws of their Athenian elders, the young lovers run away to the woods. Most of the central action of the play takes place in the woods, a fictional world not ruled by law or patriarchy but by the mischievous fairies and by desires and dreams. After a confusing, dream-like night in the woods (which the lovers may or may not remember), the lovers are welcomed back to Athens by Theseus, who has been convinced to overrule Egeus and allow them to marry according to their own wishes. Order is restored in the Athenian court, but in this case it is a new order, signified by the joint wedding of three couples, which successfully incorporates romantic love and desire with the original law and order of the state. In effect, our third phase is a synthesis or fusion of the first and second. The Athenian court authority is re-established, but it has been softened and humanized to a certain extent by the experiences of the young lovers, whose disruptive desires and fantasies are successfully incorporated back into the society.

Think about how the play might have ended differently. Hermia and Lysander could have run off into the woods and never returned, living out a different life under the sign of the fairies and their world of fantasy, dreams, and desires. Conversely, Hermia could have been scared by her night in the woods and gone back to admit her father was right all along, accepting his choice of Demetrius as her husband. Neither of these things happens, of course, and Shakespeare instead presents a comic resolution that blends elements of both worlds into his ending.

We can see the three-part structure quite clearly in the visual imagery, costumes, and settings of filmed versions of *A Midsummer Night's Dream*. Costumes and settings for the opening scenes are generally formal and signify wealth and prestige. Once we journey into the fairy world of the forest, the look and feel is completely different. The formal world of the court is replaced by shimmering moonbeams, lush overgrown vegetation, and costumes that are brightly colored, fantastical, and linked to nature rather than culture or the city. When we return to Athens at the end of the play, the visual setting and imagery usually combine elements from both the court and the forest to symbolize the merger or fusion of the two worlds.

Comedy depends on leaving audiences with a sense of closure and completeness, a feeling that things have turned out as they should. Often there are interesting things that are left unresolved or are just whisked away by the rapid *dénouements* of the comedies, and these are worth looking at as well. How much does Katharina really "believe" her own speech about wifely obedience at the end of *The Taming of the Shrew*, for example? How much do the four young lovers remember about their Midsummer's night in the woods? Does Hermia recall that Lysander has turned on her and humiliated her for being short and dark haired? Does Helena remember chasing Demetrius around like his "spaniel"? Shakespeare's comedies continue to resonate with audiences because of their ambiguities and subtexts. In a sense, Shakespeare manages to have it both ways in his comic plots. He manages to weave a perfectly contrived happy ending for his audiences, often after venturing far into potentially tragic themes and situations, and leave some lasting questions that keep vital issues unresolved and hence open to reinterpretation. Contemporary filmed versions of the comedies succeed to the extent that they recognize and bring forth these complexities.

Preview Questions: Comic Form and Structure

1. Use Northrop Frye's generic plot outline to analyze the plot of one of Shakespeare's comedies. Who is the protagonist or hero? (There may be more than one.) What obstacles stand between him (or her) and his (or her) goal or desire? How are

these obstacles overcome? Who helps the protagonist? Who hinders? Why?

2. What kind of society is established or re-established at the end of the play? Has the original society or state been changed? overthrown? By whom? And how?

3. Consider the relationship of setting to the plot. Is there a division between a civilized or cultivated world and a primitive forest or fantasy world? How are these differences represented in the play? Who journeys into the fantasy world? How are they changed by their experiences there?

4. Many of the comedies use double or multiple plots. Make a chart or table to identify the main plots and their relationships to each other in the play you are working with. Which characters are linked to or contrasted with others? How are they different? How are the characters grouped together?

The Comedies on Film

The comedies have not been nearly as popular among filmmakers as the tragedies. However, they remain immensely popular and frequently performed on the stage. In part, this may be because the comedies often work better with a live audience. Many of the comedies include physical humor, verbal banter, and staged movements (like dances) that are hard to recreate in a film environment. With a few exceptions, the great directors have favored a steady diet of tragedy, especially gravitating toward *Hamlet, Othello,* and *Macbeth.* Fortunately for our purposes, though, there have been at least a handful of relatively successful films made of the major comedies. Not only are the comedies significant in their own right, but they also foreshadow some of the themes and character types that Shakespeare would return to later in the great tragedies.

The Taming of the Shrew

The Taming of the Shrew is one of Shakespeare's earliest comedies, composed—as far as we can tell—sometime in 1590 or 1591. It is also one of the first Shakespeare plays to have been produced as a Hollywood (sound) film. In 1929, Sam Taylor adapted the play for the screen and directed Mary Pickford and Douglas Fairbanks Sr. in a relatively sophisticated and successful film. Taylor cut the Induction, along with most of the Bianca-Lucentio plot, in order to focus on Petruchio and Kate, who were played by the real-life husband and wife team of Fairbanks and Pickford. At the time, the two were Hollywood's biggest stars, and their fame certainly contributed to the film's success for United Artists. Unfortunately, Taylor's 1929 *Taming* has gone out of print and is not widely available today, although a restored version is reportedly in development and may be re-released sometime in the near future.

The *Taming of the Shrew* also forms the basis for a recent teen film, *10 Things I Hate About You* (1999). Directed by Gil Junger, *10 Things* stars Julia Stiles as Kat, refigured as a post-feminist intellectual whose bad experiences with boys have led her to swear off dating. The film's Petruchio, "Patrick Verona," is a troubled hunk from Australia played by Heath Ledger. While the film is rather loosely adapted from Shakespeare's play, and the language is rewritten as modern dialogue, *10 Things* does show the continuing resilience and adaptability of the *Taming* story for contemporary audiences. If you plan to write about *Taming of the Shrew*, it may be worth your time to rent *10 Things I Hate About You*. Lacking Shakespeare's original language, it doesn't help much with an understanding of the text of the play itself, but it is interesting to consider what *10 Things* says about the continuing relevance of controlling fathers and misrepresentation as a strategy for getting a date. The charged gender politics of Shakespeare's original plot continue to resonate even when the setting for *Taming* is moved to the contemporary suburbs.

The Taming of the Shrew
Franco Zeffirelli, Director, 1966

Elizabeth Taylor—*Katharina*	Alan Webb—*Gremio*
Richard Burton—*Petruchio*	Natasha Pyne—*Bianca*
Cyril Cusask—*Grumio*	Michael York—*Lucentio*
Michael Hordern—*Baptista*	Victor Spinetti—*Hortensio*
Alfred Lynch—*Tranio*	

Continuing the tradition established by Sam Taylor's casting, another famous real-life husband and wife team, Richard Burton and Elizabeth Taylor, appeared as Petruchio and Katharina in Franco Zeffirelli's 1966 film version of *Taming*. Their star power alone was able to propel the film to some degree of success—enough so that Zeffirelli's *Taming* would inspire a renewal of interest in Shakespeare on film, inaugurating a second major period of productivity in the late 1960s and early 1970s. The first period, in the late 1940s and early 1950s, was fuelled by Laurence Olivier and Orson Welles. Audiences in 1966 would have been unable to separate the on-screen and offscreen dramas of Burton and Taylor, whose stormy relationship was often in the headlines. For viewers at the time, Burton *was* Petruchio (his well-documented drinking just adding to the picture) and Taylor *was* Kate. Audience responses to the plot and dialogue undoubtedly would have been colored by their feelings about the stars playing the lead roles. Nearly 40 years later, our response to Zeffirelli's film can be more detached and critical, and we're in a better position to make critical inquiries into the film's take on the central issues of gender and power.

Watching Zeffirelli's film today, viewers come away with many of the same questions audiences and critics of Shakespeare's play have been debating for years. To what extent is Kate actually "tamed" by Petruchio? Is her transformation into spokeswoman for

46

domestic obedience (in her closing speech at Bianca's wedding feast) for real, or is she "playing along" with the game to help Petruchio win his bet? Has male authority triumphed over resistant femininity? Or have Kate and Petruchio "fallen in love" with one another? Although Zeffirelli transforms some of the verbal banter of the lead characters into physical comedy for the screen, his screenplay stays reasonably close to Shakespeare's original script. As you think about how you respond to and interpret Kate's speech and actions at the end of the film, you'll want to go back to the text of the play to look more closely at her lines and their implications. Certainly, Petruchio uses both physical and psychological violence on Kate to persuade her to change her behavior. The brutality of his tactics is inescapable, and the film does not shy away from dramatizing this violence. To what extent has Petruchio whipped the spirit out of Kate? How self-conscious is her transformation? Has she just learned how to play the game? Is her apparent obedience to patriarchal convention really a sophisticated form of resistance?

Despite the power and appeal of Burton and Taylor in their roles, we shound't overlook the importance of the Lucentio-Bianca plot. Shakespeare often uses the device of double or multiple plotting to reflect on a central theme or motif from several angles at the same time. Remember that Petruchio's courtship of Katharina is motivated by money (he knows he'll get a dowry of 20,000 crowns, as well as the inheritance of half of her father's lands). The theme of marriage for money appears as well in the Bianca plotline. Bianca's father insists on a signed contract from Lucentio's father before he consents to their marriage. Identity and disguise are also strongly figured themes in the Bianca story, since all of her suitors at some point are forced to woo her in disguise in order to penetrate her father's defenses. The noble Lucentio appears to Bianca as a struggling language tutor. In a reversal of the *Joe Millionaire* story, Lucentio is able to reveal to Bianca that he really is wealthy after all, a son of the Pisan aristocrat Vincentio. Shakespeare's frame tale from the Induction would seem to suggest that it's easier for a rich man to get away with playing poor for a while than for a poor man to pretend to wealth.

In an ironic reversal, Zeffirelli seems to suggest that the fair Bianca may have been playing at docility as much as her older sister Kate had been playing the shrew. We're left wondering in the final scene if she has been duping Lucentio all along since he apparently has begun to wonder as much himself. Identity, appearance, convention, money, and gender all play into the plot's complications, and not all of the strands are completely tied up in the film's fast-paced *denouement*.

Zeffirelli's set design and art direction features a carnivalesque element: Just as Lucentio arrives in Padua, a carnival begins, and throughout the film the town is convulsed by celebration and partying. This carnivalesque eruption creates an environment of misrule and parody in which social conventions are mocked and challenged. The street scenes evoke a *mélange* of Mardi Gras and the Day of the Dead, creating a vibrant and ironic subtext that places the power and authority of the legitimate leaders (the fathers) in question. While the comic closure of the play seems to put things back in order, Zeffirelli's subtexts tend to leave some of these key questions less resolved than the play's closing lines might suggest.

Analysis and Interpretation: The Taming of the Shrew

1. Why do you think Zeffirelli chooses not to include the opening frame presented in Shakespeare's "Induction"? How might the Christopher Sly frame story have been filmed? What would its inclusion add to the film? Would it change the way audiences might respond to the two main plots?

2. How does Zeffirelli use the Lucentio-Bianca plot to amplify and complicate the themes of the film? Does his use of Shakespeare's double plotting add to your understanding of the main issues in the film? How are Lucentio and Bianca different from Petruchio and Kate as they are portrayed in the film?

3. What evidence is presented in the Zeffirelli film to suggest that Katharina is joking or commiserating with Petruchio, when she delivers her famous speech on obedience at the end of the

play? Would you argue that she has been "tamed"? Or is something else going on in her relationship with Petruchio?

4. Some commentators have described the relationship between Kate and Petruchio in this film, as portrayed by Burton and Taylor, as "a childish tug-of-war for power" (Welsh 93). Others have seen a more balanced and viable marriage of wit and passion. What evidence for each view do you find in particular scenes? Which of these two views would you favor? Or would you describe the relationship in different terms?

5. Zeffirelli's *Taming* has been credited with re-establishing the viability of Shakespeare for a broader film audience and with generating a second renaissance of Shakespeare films in the late 1960s. In addition to the use of superstar actors, what elements of this film do you think contributed to its popularity at the time? How does the setting, art design, and costuming of the film contribute to its mass appeal?

A Midsummer Night's Dream

A Midsummer Night's Dream is frequently performed at summer Shakespeare festivals and remains one of the most popular of the comedies. The contrasting worlds of the Athenian court and the fairy world of the forest allow for exuberant costuming and set designs, and the magical and playful themes generally make the play an enduring favorite with audiences. The comic plot includes two pairs of young lovers, an authoritarian father who disproves of his daughter's choice in love, and a journey into the woods to escape the rule of law and patriarchy. After a series of confusions and misadventures in the forest, things are all sorted out properly in the end with three conjoined wedding ceremonies taking place at the court of Theseus, Duke of Athens. Act 5 focuses primarily on a play within a play, as the newlyweds are treated to a crude performance of the love story of "Pyramus and Thisby" put on by Bottom the weaver and a company of tradesmen.

Like many of the comedies, *A Midsummer Night's Dream* has several layers of meaning, and it rewards deeper analysis. Beneath the surface of enchanting magic and comic confusion, the play touches on several key themes and issues that connect it to later comedies, as well as to some of the tragedies. Any film or stage production wrestles with some critical questions about how to interpret and present these themes. First, consider Duke Theseus and his relationship to his bride Hippolyta. While we know Theseus and Hippolyta are about to be married, we also know that the Duke has won his wife by defeating her on the battlefield: "I wooed thee with my sword / And won thy love doing thee injuries" (1.1.16-17). Hippolyta is herself literally one of the spoils of war, and Theseus reports having injured her on the battlefield. She is both a prisoner of war and his fiancée. Queen of the Amazons, the famous tribe of women warriors, Hippolyta must have some mixed feelings about her new subjugation as wife and hostage. Actors and producers have to decide what form her resistance, if any, might take.

The subtext of male power and authority runs through the stories of the young lovers as well. All four are portrayed as utterly conventional types and in many productions the two men, Demetrius and Lysander, are presented as virtually interchangeable. The women, Hermia and Helena, are usually distinguished only by height and hair color (both referred to in the text of the play): Helena is usually tall and blonde, Hermia short and dark. None of the four is an especially deep character, and we are given little motivation for each's preference in love.

The lovers' night in the forest becomes the occasion for some of the more disconcerting subtexts to surface. As Helena chases Demetrius through the forest in 2.1, she presents herself in a pose of complete abjection: "I am your spaniel; ... / The more you beat me the more I will fawn on you" (203-4). She seems to invite and welcome both mental and physical abuse in these lines. In Act 3, Lysander, under the spell of the love-blossom turns on his lover Hermia, professing to hate her and to even consider killing her:

"What, should I hurt her, strike her, kill her dead? / Although I hate her, I'll not harm her so" (3.2.269-70).

While the four lovers do get sorted out and reconnected by morning, audiences are left to wonder how much of the emotional and physical violence of the night before remains to affect them. The play seems to suggest that love is both powerful and fickle and that passion includes elements of power, possession, and violence alongside romance and kindness. Are the four lovers in any way transformed by their experiences in the woods? Do they remember anything of that night? The text of the play does not deal explicitly with these questions, but film and stage performances have opportunities in the way they present Act 5 to evoke or suggest some of these unsettling questions.

The power struggle between Oberon and Titania, King and Queen of the Fairies, frames the stories of the human couples. Oberon and Titania are feuding over custody of a "changeling boy," and their fighting has upset the weather and the cycle of the seasons. Oberon concocts his revenge in the form of the love potion that causes Titania to fall in love with Bottom the weaver, who has himself been magically "translated" into a half-human monster with the head of an ass. As Oberon relates to Puck in 4.1, the plot works, and Oberon wins the boy through his mischievous magic. As with the other male-female relations, we see the role of power and illusion in the workings of this relationship. When she awakens, Titania asks for an explanation as she gazes upon Bottom's long-eared form: "How came these things to pass?" Oberon's only response: "Silence awhile."

Oberon explains that the Athenians will be no more affected by their misdeeds in the woods than by a bad dream: "May all to Athens back again repair, / And think no more of this night's accidents / But as the fierce vexation of a dream" (4.1.66-8). However dreams may be more powerful than he wants to admit.

A fourth subplot accompanies the "rude mechanicals" and their play within the play. While Theseus and the Athenian couples dismiss "Pyramus and Thisby" as a bad form of mindless distraction, the play as a whole tends to suggest otherwise. The world of the stage is artfully linked with the world of magic and dreams. It is as if the theater forms a link or gateway between the waking world and the fairy forest, a kind of pathway for imagination, dreams, revelry, and even magic. In *Dream*, the stage is a space upon which the libidinal and psychic energies of art and romance may find their way into the more mundane world of the waking audience. Puck's closing speech to the audience makes the link between the stage and the dream world explicit: "If we shadows have offended, / Think but this, and all is mended, / That you have but slumbered here / While these visions did appear" (5.1.418-21). The play leaves us with quite a few questions and lingering thoughts about just how powerful and transformative the shadows and slumbers of the stage may be. Like a strange dream before waking, the play is not so easily shaken off.

A Midsummer Night's Dream
Adrian Noble, Director, 1996

Lindsay Duncan—*Hippolyta*	Emily Raymond—*Helena*
Alex Jennings—*Theseus/Oberon*	Alfred Burke—*Egeus*
Desmond Barrit—*Bottom*	Kevin Doyle—*Demetrius*
Finbar Lynch—*Philostrate/Puck*	Daniel Evans—*Lysander*
Monica Dolan—*Hermia*	

William Shakespeare's A Midsummer Night's Dream
Michael Hoffman, Director, 1999

Kevin Kline—*Bottom*	Christian Bale—*Demetrius*
Michelle Pfeiffer—*Titania*	Anna Friel—*Hermia*
Stanley Tucci—*Puck*	David Straitharn—*Theseus*
Rupert Everett—*Oberon*	Sophie Marceau—*Hippolyta*
Calista Flockhart—*Helena*	Heather Parisi—*Bottom's Wife*
Dominic West—*Lysander*	

Two recent film versions of *A Midsummer Night's Dream* offer a wonderful opportunity to look at the different ways the play can be imagined and produced as a film. Adrian Noble directs a 1996 version based on the Royal Shakespeare Company stage production. This production focuses more on the language of the play (as one would expect an RSC production to do), and it employs a relatively sparse set design for the forest sequences especially. In contrast, Michael Hoffman's 1999 film of the play was produced as a Hollywood feature film, starring well-known film actors (Kevin Kline, Michele Pfeiffer, and Stanley Tucci, among others), and is quite lavish in its locations and set design. While the Noble film aims to adapt to film a production largely imagined for the stage, the Hoffman film clearly aims to translate *A Midsummer Night's Dream* into the language of the Hollywood feature film.

The Noble/RSC film adds one key element not originally a part of Shakespeare's play. The film opens in a young boy's bedroom, and we are expected to understand the main action of the story as his dream or nightmare. Not only is the film understood to take place in this unnamed boy's dream world, but he is also present throughout as a witness or audience member. At times the actors almost stumble over him, but we are apparently supposed to understand that he is invisible. To some extent, he represents the audience, encouraged by Puck to perceive the whole thing as if it were a dream. In another scene, he plays with the actors literally as his puppet show, in a sequence that seems to equate him more closely with the playwright or director (pulling the strings, literally) than with the audience/dreamer. The heavily sexualized plot, especially the Titania-Bottom sex scenes, seems out of place for a young boy's dream. Nonetheless, the use of this device works to put an interesting spin on the relationship of drama and art to life.

The artistic direction of the Noble/RSC film blends elements of surrealism with more traditional stagecraft. One of the major visual motifs is the umbrella, which at certain times seems to come from Mary Poppins (the fairies travel about using umbrellas as magical locomotion), and at others to come from the surrealist imagery of painter René Magritte. The world of the fairy forest is a simple stage, bordering a lake or lagoon, decorated with hundreds of bare light bulbs. These fairy/firefly bulbs are for the most part the only decoration on the stage, with the exception of the umbrellas and a few simple props. The simple imagery of the set seems to suggest a non-localized dream world rather than a specific geographical place. Throughout, Noble uses doorways, false walls and doors, and other partitions to suggest a surreal, two-dimensional place in the imagination, a nowhere that could be almost anywhere. Occasional special effects are used to remind viewers that the film is to be understood as happening in the boy's dreams. Strange shifts in perspective and point of view, tilted cameras, and bright primary colors all contribute to this effect.

Despite its location in a youthful dream, however, the Noble/RSC film includes more of the unsettling and provocative lines than the Hoffman version. The fairies are more sexualized, more deviant, perhaps more threatening. The gender politics are foregrounded almost from the very beginning: Hippolyta slaps Theseus in the opening scene, punishing him physically for his authoritarian and heartless application of Athenian law. Theseus sides with Egeus and demands that Hermia agree to marry Demetrius instead of Lysander or be punished with either death or banishment to a convent. In contrast, the Hoffman film includes only a mildly scolding look from Hippolyta to Theseus in place of the more obvious slap in the face.

Michael Hoffman's film seems intended to introduce the play to a broader audience of film viewers. The actors include recognizable film stars Kevin Kline (as Bottom; Kline is actually an accomplished Shakespearean actor and has played Hamlet, among other major roles), Michelle Pfeiffer (Titania), Rupert Everett (Oberon), and even Stanley Tucci as Puck. For viewers who know the play, a certain amount of the charm of this film comes from watching familiar actors play their sometimes miscast parts (Tucci as a balding fairy, for example; or Calista Flockhart as a continually exasperated Helena). Watching these performances in direct contrast to the RSC acting, one can see the distinctly different styles of voicing and gesturing akin to both stage and film styles of acting.

Hoffman adds a bit of resonance and back story to the character of Bottom. Kline's character is given a wife, who does not approve of his "dreaming" and acting pretensions. He is an object of social ridicule and scorn: Two boys douse him with red wine as he rehearses in his white linen suit. Hoffman seems to extend Shakespeare's insights into the world of the theater to offer at least the outlines of a new subplot, focused on Bottom, showing the consequences of choosing a life of stage acting and illusion over a life of practical "reality." There's a certain amount of sentimentality in the treatment of Bottom as an object of pathos in Hoffman's film, but it does contribute to a way of thinking about the role of actors in the "make-believe" that comprises the theater.

There is one last surprise in the way Hoffman presents the "Pyramus and Thisby" play at the end. While the Athenian audience mocks the players by maintaining their sophisticated ironic poses, the actor playing Thisby pulls off his wig and speaks as a man (out of costume as Thisby), delivering the badly written lines so well that even Theseus is visibly moved. This brief scene seems also to extend some of Shakespeare's themes about the power of theater—it turns out that this Thisbe is actually a fantastic actor, able to move even the most jaded audience to tears through the sheer power of his acting.

In contrast to the Noble/RSC film version, the set design and locations for the Hoffman film are detailed and lush. "Athens" is actually Mount Athena, somewhere in Italy (backed by operatic music throughout); the forest-fairy world is lush, Victorian, vegetative, and sensual. The film works very hard to realize the most fantastic illusions about what the forest world and the court might look like. The luscious vegetation and neo-Victorian scenery is sometimes undercut by the slapstick bicycle chases, culminating in a completely over-the-top scene in which Helena and Hermia engage in nearly naked mud wrestling. The foolishness and pettiness of "these mortals" is certainly brought forth in obvious ways in the film. Nonetheless, *A Midsummer Night's Dream* proves to work effectively as light-hearted Hollywood fare.

Analysis and Interpretation: A Midsummer Night's Dream

1. The Noble and Hoffman films use differently edited scripts of the play. In Hoffman's screenplay, one notable edit cuts the lines in which Theseus reveals that he has won Hippolyta as his bride by defeating her on the battlefield. What other differences do you see in the lines and scenes each play includes or deletes? What does each film choose to emphasize? What does each edit out or de-emphasize? Which edited version of the play do you prefer? Why?

2. Adrian Noble's film adds an element not present in Shakespeare's play: the young boy who is both dreaming and participating in the events. How does this device change your relationship to the events of the film? Why would a director choose to portray the play literally as a dream?

3. Michael Hoffman gives a deeper presence and back story to the character of Bottom. What does he add to Shakespeare's play in order to do this? How does the emphasis on Bottom and the "rude mechanicals" shift the thematic emphasis of the film?

4. Compare the acting styles in the Noble/RSC film with those in the Hoffman film. What differences in technique and presentation do you notice? Which techniques and styles, in your opinion, are most effective on film? Why? How does the technology of filmmaking change the way actors present their lines and characters?

5. Adrian Noble's set design is minimalist compared to Hoffman's. What visual effects and props does Noble use to create his film's story world? Is his set and visual direction more appropriate or successful in presenting a dream world?

6. How does each of these two films address issues of gender and power? How does the mirroring of themes in the four different couples' plots work to suggest a particular view of the nature

of love and romance? Does either film challenge contemporary views of love and romance?

7. To what extent are Shakespeare's assumptions about the power of theater also true of cinema as well? Do either of these films comment in any way, implicitly or explicitly, on the power of cinema to transform audiences?

Much Ado About Nothing

Much Ado About Nothing is one of a group of three romantic comedies written between 1598 and 1600. Bevington describes *Much Ado*, along with *Twelfth Night* and *As You Like It*, as "the culmination of Shakespeare's exuberant, philosophical, and festive vein in comedy" (219). The play puts two romantic couples and their stories in dramatic contrast. In one story, Claudio, a soldier who has done well in military service to Don Pedro, returns from war and turns his attention to finding a wife in the person of Hero. Hero is the devoted and obedient daughter of Leonato, the Governor of Messina (the Sicilian city-state where the play takes place). The contrasting plot revolves around Beatrice and Benedick. Both have sworn to remain unmarried, and each maintains a studious pose of aloof nonconformity and professed cynicism about the opposite sex. Beatrice and Benedick are rich and fully developed characters (unlike many of the lovers in the comedies, who tend to be predictable stereotypes), and the charged verbal exchanges between them form the center of the play's energy and humor. The "merry war" between them echoes back to *The Taming of the Shrew*, but in *Much Ado* the two characters are more evidently equal matches for one another. The power dynamic is balanced, and without the element of physical and emotional domination found in the earlier play.

As you might expect, both of these couples end up together, planning to be married, at the end of the play. As is generally the case in the comic plots, the ending re-establishes closure and order and manages somehow to resolve the many conflicts and problems that have surfaced along the way. So what are the conflicts and obstacles that come between the two pairs of lovers, and how are they overcome?

In the case of Claudio and Hero, the obstacles to their romantic union come in the form of the rumors and false perceptions created by the play's villain, Don John, and his henchmen, Conrade and Borachio. They manage to mislead Claudio on two different occasions and they come very close to completely ruining his life, let alone his chances with Hero. In the first situation, they convince Claudio that Don Pedro is courting Hero for himself rather than on Claudio's behalf. At the masked ball in Act 2, Don John talks to Claudio, pretending to think that he is speaking to Benedick (the characters are wearing masks). Claudio responds as Benedick, and Don John tells him that Don Pedro "is enamored on Hero" and asks "Benedick" to "dissuade him from her; she is no equal for his birth" (2.1.158-9). Claudio's soliloquy shortly afterward indicates that he has completely fallen for the trap, immediately believing the lie that Don Pedro is out for himself rather than helping his friend:

> Thus answer I in the name of Benedick,
> But hear these ill news with the ears of Claudio.
> 'Tis certain so. The Prince woos for himself.
> Friendship is constant in all other things
> Save in the office and affairs of love;
> Therefore all hearts in love use their own tongues.
> Let every eye negotiate for itself
> And trust no agent; for beauty is a witch
> Against whose charms faith melteth into blood.
> This is an accident of hourly proof,
> Which I mistrusted not. Farewell therefore Hero!
> (2.1.166-76)

Claudio's willingness to accept false rumors about his friend Don Pedro (and to give up on Hero) suggests something close to a tragic flaw in him. He is quick to accept rumors of the worst, hasty in his willingness to abandon good faith and believe that people are base and self-serving at heart. Claudio's rush to judgment is of course contradicted by the facts just a few moments later. Don Pedro has won the heart of Hero, not for himself, as Claudio fears, but for Claudio. Claudio will get his Hero after all, and the marriage has the blessing of Hero's father, Leonato, to boot.

Claudio's rush to harsh judgment works against him a second time, in even more dramatic and potentially tragic fashion. With the aid of Borachio, Don John orchestrates a little performance in which Claudio is led to believe that Hero is having an affair. Claudio witnesses a woman he thinks is Hero making love with Borachio at her balcony window. The whole scene has been arranged ahead of time, as we know, and it is not Hero but her serving-woman Margaret that Claudio spies in Borachio's embrace. Nonetheless, Claudio is again prepared to think the worst and he proceeds to attack Hero at their wedding altar the next day, accusing her of lying about her virginity and honor. He angrily gives his intended bride back to her father:

> There, Leonato, take her back again.
> Give not this rotten orange to your friend;
> She's but a sign and semblance of her honor.
> Behold how like a maid she blushes here!
> Oh, what authority and show of truth
> Can cunning sin cover itself withal!
> Comes not that blood as modest evidence
> To witness simple virtue? Would you not swear,
> All you that see her, that she were a maid,
> By these exterior shows? But she is none:
> She knows the heat of a luxurious bed.
> Her blush is guiltiness, not modesty.
>   (4.1.30-41)

This scene, in which Claudio publicly humiliates both Hero and her father, Leonato, is perhaps the most intense and emotionally violent scene in the play. Seeing his daughter's reputation destroyed, Leonato expresses a wish to die ("Hath no man's dagger here a point for me?"). Like Claudio, Leonato is also willing to believe the false rumors about his daughter ("Would the two princes lie and Claudio lie?"), and in his ranting he actually wishes her dead. Only through the intercession of Benedick and the Friar is Leonato calmed down enough to pause in his indictment of his daughter.

This segment of the story carries some eerie foreshadowing of *Othello*. Claudio seems to be obsessed with images of women's sexuality as threatening and volatile ("beauty is a witch") and he is easily led into destructive fantasies ("she knows the heat of a luxurious bed"). His response when his faith is tested is to lash out in violence. If not for the benign interventions of his friends (and the incredible forgiveness of Hero), Claudio would doom himself to a life of fretted isolation.

Two key things happen in the story to return the play to its comic course. First, Constable Dogberry and his watchmen manage through lucky chance to discover and unravel the plot laid by Don John and Borachio, forcing them to confess that Claudio has been set up and that Hero is completely innocent. Second, Leonato, Hero, and the Friar concoct a way to teach Claudio a lesson while getting him back together with Hero after all. They convince Claudio that Hero has died of shame, and after forcing him to perform public penance at her tomb, get him to agree to marry Antonio's daughter in recompense. This fictive daughter is then unveiled as Hero herself, not dead after all ("She died, my lord, but whiles her slander lived"). The play manages to use Don John as the villainous scapegoat, and his reported capture at the very end restores a sense of poetic justice to the story. Nonetheless, *Much Ado*, like *A Midsummer Night's Dream*, unleashes some disturbing and potentially tragic energies that its hasty resolution cannot entirely contain.

While the movement of the Claudio-Hero story provides the basic plot mechanism driving the play forward, the relationship of Beatrice and Benedick provides its emotional and psychological center. Beatrice and Benedick are among the most compelling and memorable characters in all the comedies. They are smart, self-aware, realistic, and perceptive. Where Claudio is consumed with the appearance of things, his counterpart Benedick is quick to see through to the underlying truths. Benedick is convinced of Hero's innocence throughout, for example. Beatrice and Benedick are both good judges of character, shrewd observers of the people and events around them.

Beatrice and Benedick stand at the opposite end of the spectrum from Claudio and Hero. They are both too smart to buy into conventional wisdom and their relationship is described by Leonato as "a kind of merry war" (1.1.57). The play gives us some hints that they have been romantically involved with one another in the past and that the results were not good (see 2.1, especially lines 265-68). They have both grown so proudly attached to their aloof single postures that they have to be tricked by their friends into admitting their love for each other. Benedick expresses his lofty expectations for a mate in the following: "but till all graces be in one woman, one woman shall not come in my grace" (2.3.29-31). Benedick's all-or-nothing standards are shared by Beatrice. When her uncle, Leonato, expresses his hope "to see you one day fitted with a husband," her response is "Not till God make men of some other metal than earth" (2.1.53-6).

The process through which these two anti-romantics are drawn together forms one of the central dynamics of the plot of *Much Ado*. Their direct exchanges sometimes take place masked, so that they know they are talking to each other but pretend not to. They are manipulated by their friends, who artfully arrange staged performances for the benefit of the eavesdropping protagonists. Only when each is let in on the secret of the other's feelings does either one of them openly admit to themselves that they do indeed feel something for the other. But clearly Beatrice and Benedick possess a mature self-awareness that Claudio and Hero lack. Beatrice and Benedick are able to see through social convention in order to develop a more authentic intimacy.

Much Ado About Nothing
Kenneth Branagh, Director, 1993

Denzel Washington—*Don Pedro*

Richard Briers—*Leonato*

Brian Blessed—*Antonio*

Kenneth Branagh—*Benedick*

Emma Thompson—*Beatrice*

Robert Sean Leonard—*Claudio*

Kate Beckinsale—*Hero*

Imelda Staunton—*Margaret*

Keanu Reaves—*Don John*

Gerard Horan—*Borachio*

Richard Clifford—*Conrade*

Michael Keaton—*Dogberry*

Kenneth Branagh's 1993 film of *Much Ado* is one of a select few Shakespeare films to achieve both critical and popular success. Branagh's acting, in the role of Benedick, opposite Emma Thompson's strong and self-assured Beatrice, contributes greatly to the film. Denzel Washington and Keanu Reaves add box-office drawing power, and Michael Keaton as Dogberry brings an element of comic genius and charm. The film is set in a lush Italian villa, which adds an aura of earthy summer sensuality to the film that enhances the already vibrant eroticism of the play itself.

One interesting formal element in Branagh's film is the use of the song ("Sigh no more, ladies, sigh no more") as a framing device and motif throughout the film. This song appears in Shakespeare's text in Act 2, Scene 3, but Branagh moves it to a more prominent place. As the film begins, the words to this song appear sequentially on an otherwise blank screen as they are read by Emma Thompson in voice-over. The first image we see is an unfinished watercolor painting of an Italian villa. The camera pans left to reveal the actual villa in the distance beyond the edge of the painting. The residents of Leonato's Messina are lolling about in the summer sun, enjoying a late afternoon picnic. As the camera continues its slow pan left, we finally come to rest on Beatrice (Thompson) sitting in a tree reading the song to the gathered audience. The lines of the song form an effective sound bridge that crosses from offscreen to on-screen space.

A color still from Branagh's film appears in the Bevington text. Plate 12 shows Beatrice (Thompson) and Benedick (Branagh) in an animated conversation from Act 5, Scene 2. In this scene, Beatrice has come to ask Benedick whether or not he has followed through on his promise to challenge Claudio. To her inquiry into what has passed between them, Benedick replies, "Only foul words; and thereupon I will kiss you." But she turns it back on him: "Foul words is but foul wind, and foul wind is but foul breath, and foul breath is noisome; therefore I will depart unkissed" (5.2.48-52). The image shows Branagh's use of the window to frame the shot, as well as the verdant Italian countryside in the background.

It's also important to pay attention to Branagh's use of two of the primary dramatic devices in the play: masks and eaves-dropping. The masked ball presented in Act 2 contains numerous instances of willful as well as accidental misrecognition as the characters are all masked. Both Beatrice and Benedick are done in by their friends who intentionally stage conversations they want the protagonists to overhear.

Analysis and Interpretation: **Much Ado About Nothing**

1. David Bevington writes (in the editor's introduction) that "it is the search for candor and self-awareness in relationships with others, the quest for honesty and respect beneath conventional outward appearances, that provides the journey in this play." To what extent can that interpretation also be applied to Branagh's film? Which characters participate in this journey? Through what process do they succeed (or fail) in their search for self-awareness?

2. Some reviewers have commented that Branagh makes Claudio more sympathetic to audiences than does the original play. Do you agree? What changes has Branagh made in the script and

in the presentation of the story that would support the thesis that he wants to present a more likable Claudio?

3. Find an example of a scene where a character is masked or where one character is eavesdropping on a conversation. How does Branagh handle these scenes? What functions does the device of the mask or overhearing serve in this film? What do characters learn or discover when they are hidden or disguised? How do their discoveries affect them?

4. Re-read the complete text of the song that appears in the play in Act 2, Scene 3 (lines 61-76). How do you explicate these lines? When Branagh uses them as a kind of epigraph to his film, what themes does it emphasize? Does the film support the statement that "men were deceivers ever"?

Twelfth Night; or, What You Will

The title of *Twelfth Night* refers to the twelfth night of Christmas, celebrated in Shakespeare's time as The Feast of the Epiphany (January 6). The twelve days of Christmas were a time of celebration and revelry, culminating in the carnival atmosphere of Twelfth Night itself. As in some of the other comedies, the seasonal revelry offers an occasion to turn authority or convention on its head and for fools to become philosophers and kings. This dramatic reversal is perhaps most evident in the stories of Feste and Malvolio. In *Twelfth Night*, Feste is a traveling minstrel-fool who entertains the locals with songs and wit. He takes part in a plot to undo Malvolio, the kill-joy steward of Lady Olivia's household who is always enforcing quiet and decorum. Feste ends up pretending to be a priest while Malvolio is locked up in darkness and accused of being insane. Feste often seems to be the sanest, wisest person in the play, even though he is a homeless beggar. His role prefigures other wise fools, most notably the Fool in *King Lear*. In Bevington's description, Feste represents "an inversion of appearance and reality whereby many of the world's ordinary pursuits can be seen to be ridiculous."

A related inversion of appearances takes place when Viola disguises herself as "Cesario" in order to infiltrate the world of

Duke Orsino's court. Disguised as a man, Viola serves as an emissary of Orsino, pleading his case to Olivia, who continues to rebuff his every advance. In the course of this plot, things get very confused: Olivia falls in love with "Cesario," a woman she thinks is a man. Viola, pretending to be "Cesario" falls in love with Orsino. And Orsino, pining away melodramatically for Olivia, confides in and befriends "Cesario," not realizing that his young friend is a woman. The play presents a modern concept of gender as appearance and convention as it seeks to confuse and then unravel all the misdirected desires of its main characters. As in most of the comedies, the couples are sorted out into conventionally heterosexual couples by the end (thanks to the appearance of Viola's identical twin brother Sebastian). At the same time, the homoerotic subtexts are strongly present, available to be either exploited or avoided in performance and film.

Twelfth Night
Trevor Nunn, Director, 1996

Helena Bonham Carter— *Olivia*	Nicholas Farrell—*Antonio*
Nigel Hawthorne—*Malvolio*	Imelda Staunton—*Maria*
Imogen Stubbs—*Viola*	Toby Stephens—*Duke Orsino*
Ben Kingsley—*Feste*	
Mel Smith—*Sir Toby Belch*	Richard E. Grant—*Sir Andrew Aguecheek*
Steven Mackintosh— *Sebastian*	

Only one feature film of *Twelfth Night* has been made: Trevor Nunn's 1996 stylish version, filmed on the rocky Cornwall coastline. Nunn sets his film somewhere in the early 19th century, with uniforms and costumes that suggest a time frame somewhere around the Napoleonic wars. Nunn's Feste, played by Ben Kingsley, functions like a chorus or narrator. His songs frame the beginning and end of the film, and Kingsley occasionally makes direct eye contact with the camera/viewer, even winking at us at the end of the film. Kingsley's Feste brings a note of melancholy existentialism to the film: His willowy songs evoke the passing of time and the coming of death. His urgings to seize the day come more from old-age resignation than from youthful exuberance.

In the realist medium of film, it's somewhat hard to believe that Viola (Imogen Stubbs) could be mistaken for a man. (It's worth remembering that Shakespeare's Viola would have been played by an adolescent male, hence "Cesario" would appear onstage as a man pretending to be a woman pretending to be a man.) There are a few moments when characters flirt with same-sex kisses or embraces, but the film studiously, and perhaps fastidiously, avoids anything more than a close call among the gender-confused pairs. Nonetheless, Nunn's actors manage to bring both humor and pathos to their roles, and the film manages to find a balance between the humor and the darker philosophical elements of the play.

A color image from Nunn's *Twelfth Night* can be seen in the Bevington text. Plate 13 shows the four lovers in their festive wedding clothes at the very end of the film. Olivia (Helena Bonham Carter) is on the left, with Sebastian (Steven Mackintosh), Viola (Imogen Stubbs, now in women's clothes), and Orsino (Toby Stephens), left to right. The ending sequence of *Twelfth Night* shows both the establishment of the new society and the departure (or exile) of those characters that have no place in this new society. Nunn intercuts scenes from the wedding dance (in the lavish costumes seen in Plate 13) with shots of individual characters departing the world of Olivia's household. One by one, Antonio, Malvolio, and Maria depart into the distance, suitcase in hand. Malvolio has vowed revenge and leaves to escape the indignities he has experienced at the hands of Maria and Sir Toby. Maria leaves, presumably at Olivia's request, disgraced for her role in the sinister plot to abuse Malvolio. Antonio leaves simply because there's no place for him in the new order: His Sebastian is now linked to Olivia. The film's closing sequence shows how the happy world of the two couples establishes itself by banishing certain others who no longer have a place in it. Finally, Feste himself, who has served as our narrator and whose song (" For the rain it raineth every day") accompanies the film's ending sequence, gives us a wink, shoulders his satchel and lute, and walks off down the hill and out of the frame.

Analysis and Interpretation: Twelfth Night

1. What is the relationship between friendship and romantic love in Nunn's film? Do the characters discover, as Bevington suggests, that friendship is the best basis for romantic and sexual love? How do the two main plots/couples compare and contrast on this issue? Is Orsino's attraction to "Cesario"/Viola different from Olivia's attraction to "Cesario"/Sebastian? Why or why not?

2. Explicate the songs sung by Feste at the beginning and end of the film. How does each relate to the major themes of the play? What role does Kingsley's Feste play in the world of *Twelfth Night*? What is he doing there, and how does he influence people or events?

3. The Malvolio subplot involves manipulation and deceit, much like Don John's treatment of Claudio in *Much Ado*. Who tricks Malvolio and why? Why does their plot succeed? Are we supposed to feel that Malvolio "gets his due"? Why or why not? What kind of justice is served by his comeuppance?

4. How does the setting and scenery of the film contribute to its thematic feel and atmosphere? What effect does the rocky coastline have on certain scenes? How else is setting and *mise-en-scene* used to create an emotional effect?

CHAPTER 3

The Histories

As we move from the comedies to the histories, we enter a very different world. Unlike the comedies, whose sources come from literary tradition, folklore, and popular culture, the history plays are based on real events and historical figures. More precisely, the history plays are based on historical sources, primarily Holinshed's *Chronicles* and Hall's *Union of the Two Noble and Illustre Families of Lancaster and York*. Shakespeare was a dramatist and not a historian, but he found in English history a rich vein of dramatic conflict and dynastic struggle to mine and refine for the stage.

In the history plays, we enter a world of politics, warfare, conflict, and violence. The themes that emerge in the histories concern the nature of kingship and political authority, the rules of succession and the right to the crown, the shape of the political state, and the importance of social order and hierarchy. While there are isolated moments of humor and romance in the history plays, they are generally darker and more serious in tone, as one would expect, than the comedies.

The Importance of History in Elizabethan England

Shakespeare's history plays form two groups of four plays (tetralogies), collectively covering the period known as the Wars of the Roses, which lasted from about 1398 until 1485. (See the end of this chapter for a chronology of the history plays.) Two other historical plays, *King John* and *Henry VIII*, are not directly a part of this sequence. It's important to remember that Shakespeare was writing about events relatively far in the past even in his own day. The Wars of the Roses ended with Henry Tudor's victory over

Richard III at the Battle of Bosworth, in 1485—more than a century before Shakespeare's history plays were written in the 1590s. This would be roughly equivalent to an author today writing a series of plays about the period from before the American Civil War up through World War I. By the time Shakespeare wrote about them, the historical events of the Wars of the Roses had already been at least partially transformed into myths and legends. Since then, Shakespeare's plays themselves have come to color our view of the people and events of those times.

Why would audiences in Shakespeare's day have been interested in history as a subject for drama? We know that the English history play enjoyed a period of great popularity in the 1590s, and that Shakespeare was one of several authors developing major sequences of history plays for the theaters of the day. In part this popularity was related to the status of England itself in the political world of its own day. With its defeat of the Spanish Armada in 1588, England began to assume an unprecedented position of ascendancy on the world political stage. The nation entered a period of flourishing patriotism and national pride, and one outgrowth of this was a desire to explore the historical developments and events that had brought England to its present prominence and relative stability.

At the same time, political conflicts and religious issues were simmering beneath the surface, and there was an element of propaganda to a literary genre that justified and naturalized the existing Elizabethan political order. Catholic loyalists continued to resist the tide of the Protestant Reformation. Queen Elizabeth herself had no direct heir, leaving the question of succession in doubt. Indeed, less than 40 years after her death, the nation would again slide into civil war and political turmoil, so there was something important at stake in writing (and rewriting) history in order to celebrate and justify the existing regime. Many in Shakespeare's audiences would be able to draw lessons and parallels for their own times from the stories played out on the stage before them. To that extent, the Wars of the Roses and the history plays served as cautionary tales for a nation enjoying a period of prosperity and stability that many knew might not last forever. The moment was filled with ambivalent possibility, and Shakespeare's contemporaries and his audiences looked with renewed interest at the recent past in an effort to understand their present.

Interpreting the Past

When Shakespeare and his contemporaries looked back at the history of the previous two centuries, they had two frameworks through which to interpret the past. The first of these was what might be called the medieval or providential view of history, in which people and events were seen as players in a grand, divine plan. The Wars of the Roses, in this view, were part of a divine process of punishment and restitution brought about by the arrogance and selfishness of the English people. This was generally the view put forth by the "official" historians and chroniclers of the day, whose rhetorical purpose would have been to legitimate the Tudor dynastic lineage and to glorify the Queen and her government. However Shakespeare's audiences might also have taken a second, more modern view. To them, history might have been more human than divine—a process driven by rhetoric, power, contingency, and luck more than by providential design. In the history plays, we often see these two views portrayed simultaneously, and the dramatic tension in the plays themselves often comes from the inability to choose between them. History is reworked by Shakespeare to make it interesting as theater, and this usually means presenting a narrative that can be read in multiple ways.

This ambiguity is further complicated when we shift our attention to modern films based on the history plays. Shakespeare was already re-interpreting the events of the past through his own experience and social context. A modern film adds a third layer: that of the times in which the film itself was made. One of the two films of *Richard III* discussed in this chapter, for example, makes this historical layering explicit. Richard Loncraine's 1995 film uses Nazi-era uniforms and imagery to visually link King Richard

III to Hitler and the fascist movements of the 1930s. Clearly Shakespeare could not have anticipated the horrors of the 20th century, but Loncraine's use of visual iconography from the Nazi era suggests ways in which King Richard's political theater and rhetoric might be seen as a precursor to more familiar recent forms of mass media and power politics. Even when filmmakers are less explicit than Loncraine in doing so, their films inevitably project their own era's struggles and concerns onto the dramatic conflicts in the plays.

Preview Questions: The English History Plays

1. How do the history plays represent history as a literary and dramatic subject? What types of events do the history plays chronicle?

2. Who are the primary characters in the history plays? What qualities and values do they embody?

3. What dramatic conflicts drive the actions of the history plays? What seems to be at stake in characters' actions and words?

4. What evidence in the plays supports or suggests a view of history as the enactment of providence or God's plan? What evidence undercuts or counters this view?

5. It's often said that the purpose of studying history is to avoid repeating the mistakes of the past. What evidence suggests a didactic or pedagogical purpose in the history plays?

6. How are contemporary ideas about history like or unlike the ideas presented in the plays? How has our theory of history changed? Do you see any modern parallels to events or characters in the histories? What events or time periods have been the subjects of modern history plays (or films)?

The Histories on Film

The two history plays that have been the primary focus of modern filmmakers form an interesting contrast. *Henry V* stands as a triumphant and heroic conclusion to the sequence of four plays that begins with *Richard II* and includes the first and second parts of

Henry IV. After decades of civil war, Henry's military victory over the French at Agincourt (in 1415) cemented his authority and ended the civil strife, at least for a time. In many ways, Henry is portrayed as a model king. But if Henry V is Shakespeare's most heroic king, certainly Richard III is his most villainous. The plot of *Richard III* traces Richard of Gloucester's murderous rise to power and the throne at the expense of all who stand in his way. As clearly as Henry V is king as hero, Richard III is king as anti-hero. Where Henry V concludes one tetralogy on a high note, Richard III concludes the other with a rapid degeneration into violence and chaos.

Perhaps it is these extremes, and the fact that both of these plays are focused more clearly on a single central character than many of the other histories, which have made these plays popular for film versions. *Richard III* was filmed by Laurence Olivier in 1955 in a version that for four decades stood as the definitive performance. Another film version of *Richard III* was not attempted until 1995, when Ian McKellen and Richard Loncraine made a visually striking version set in a fascist 1930s context. *Henry V* has been the subject of two major feature films: Laurence Olivier's 1944 production, often seen as a patriotic work of wartime propaganda, and Kenneth Branagh's darker and more ambiguous 1989 version.

Richard III

Representing both the end of the story of the Wars of the Roses and the end of Shakespeare's first English history tetralogy, *Richard III* raises important questions relevant to the history plays as a whole. As one of the most ruthless, Machiavellian figures in any of the plays, Richard Gloucester (later King Richard III) can be seen as both a type and an individual. As he murders and manipulates his way to the throne, we wonder to what extent we are watching a modern psychological drama and to what extent we're seeing a medieval allegory. Is Richard an allegorical character, a figure whose evil is so complete and predetermined that his eventual death cleanses the whole national landscape, clearing the way for a fresh start in the person of Henry VII (Henry Tudor)? Is his physical deformity an outward symbol of some curse or predestined role? Or is he a modern villain instead, a master of political rhetoric and theater, whose major mistakes can be read as miscalculations rather than as divine retribution?

Richard III
Laurence Olivier, Director, 1955

Cedric Hardwicke— *King Edward IV*	Mary Kerridge— *Queen Elizabeth*
Laurence Olivier— *Richard Gloucester/Richard III*	Claire Bloom— *Lady Anne*
Ralph Richardson— *Duke of Buckingham*	Andrew Cruikshank— *Sir Robert Brackenbury*
John Gielgud— *George, Duke of Clarence*	Clive Morton— *Anthony, Earl of Rivers*

Richard III
Richard Loncraine, Director, 1995

Ian McKellen— *Gloucester/Richard III*	Kristin Scott Thomas— *Lady Anne*
Annette Bening— *Queen Elizabeth*	John Wood— *King Edward IV*
Jim Broadbent— *Duke of Buckingham*	Maggie Smith— *Duchess of York*
Robert Downey, Jr.— *Anthony, Earl of Rivers*	Adrian Dunbar— *Sir James Tyrrel*
Nigel Hawthorne— *George, Duke of Clarence*	

Because Shakespeare gives plausible weight to either of these interpretations, actors and filmmakers have had considerable room to develop their own portrayals of Richard and his story. As viewers of these films, we are granted an unusual kind of intimacy with our anti-hero. Both Laurence Olivier and Ian McKellen, in their acting performances, use direct eye contact with the camera to draw us into their world and to give us glimpses into Richard's thoughts and motives that none of the other characters in the drama could have. Under both Olivier's and Loncraine's direction, the camera often follows Richard around during key soliloquies, and we often are visually aligned with his point of view during the action in important sequences. Olivier makes brilliant use of a set in which we frequently stand with Richard at a window or on a balcony, overlooking the main action while we overhear Richard's musings and commentary on what is taking place.

In Shakespeare's play, the famous opening soliloquy ("Now is the winter of our discontent / Made glorious summer by this son of York...") quickly establishes Richard's character as it builds the audience's sense of intimacy with him, however unsavory he may be as a main character. Explaining that he is "not shaped for sportive tricks," our Richard vows instead "to prove a villain." "I am subtle, false, and treacherous," he tells us, revealing before we are 40 lines into the play his plan to set his brothers Clarence and King Edward (IV), against one another. Following quickly on the heels of this, the second major scene of the play contains what has to stand as one of the most improbable courtship scenes in all of Shakespeare. Having killed her husband (Prince Edward, son of King Henry VI), Richard now woos Lady Anne as they stand over her late husband's corpse. "He that bereft thee, lady, of thy husband / Did it to help thee to a better husband" (1.2.141-2). "'Twas thy heavenly face that set me on," Richard asserts. He offers to let her kill him in revenge; he offers to kill himself if she wishes. By the end of the scene, he has placed an engagement ring on her finger. As she, her dead husband, and the pallbearers exit, we are again alone with Richard. "Was ever woman in this humor wooed?" he asks. Dumbfounded, we are inclined to answer aloud: No, never.

The character of Richard does not develop or unfold so much as it explodes onto the stage in Shakespeare's play. Hovering ominously in the background (and sometimes the foreground) of the previous plays, he now takes center stage as a fully formed villain. Few of Shakespeare's plays open as quickly or starkly as *Richard III.* How do filmmakers work to achieve similar effects in their opening moments?

Olivier opens his 1955 film with a vibrant coronation scene. As the new king Edward IV is crowned and cheered, Richard looks on from the wings. As soon as the royal procession moves off down the street, the camera turns back toward Richard. A heavy door opens slowly to show the now-empty throne room and we follow the camera's movement in, where Richard (now alone) addresses his opening lines directly to us. Sustained, direct eye contact links us with him, and for most of the rest of the film our point of view aligns closely with his.

Richard Loncraine and Ian McKellen (1995) insert their own sequence prior to the coronation scene. King Henry VI and his son Prince Edward are at their battle headquarters at Tewkesbury (the military uniforms and equipment serve to situate the scene somewhere in the late 1930s). A message comes over the tickertape: "Richard Gloucester is at hand. He holds his course toward Tewkesbury." As Edward sits down to his dinner, a heavy vibration begins to rattle his wine glass. A tank crashes through the wall into the room and armed men in gas masks rush him, killing him with machine gun fire and a final bullet between the eyes. We cut to King Henry, saying what he knows will be his final prayers. Still wearing a gas mask, Richard's face is hidden, but we immediately recognize his ambling limp and useless left arm. His loud breathing in the mask cannot help but remind us of another legendary film villain—Darth Vader. Killing the king with a single shot to the back of the head, Richard (McKellen) pulls off his mask as the film's title marches across the screen in large blood-red block letters.

75

We move to a sumptuous celebration of the new King Edward IV's coronation. Following some music and dancing, Richard addresses the assembled celebrants from the microphone. A color still from this scene is printed in the Bevington text; see Plate 15. As he speaks the opening lines of his famous soliloquy, the camera closes in on his mouth (suggesting, perhaps, the power of his rhetoric). Suddenly, the tone and scene shift and we find ourselves at the urinal in the men's room. The second half of Richard's opening speech is spoken in deeply sarcastic tones as he empties his bladder. As he washes his hands he continues to speak, evidently addressing his own reflection in the mirror. Suddenly, he catches our eye (the camera's) in the mirror, and startlingly, turns to speak directly to us: "...and therefore, since I cannot prove a lover / ... I am determined to prove a villain." Much as Olivier's camera draws us into a forced intimacy with his Richard, so too does Loncraine's washroom sequence place us squarely and immediately into a private space that only we and Richard share. Both Olivier's and Loncraine's opening sequences can be seen as effective cinematic adaptations of the dramatic soliloquy used so effectively by Shakespear—both to characterize Richard and at the same time to establish an intimate relationship between the arch-villain and his audience.

Richard is in fact both an actor and a director as the story unfolds. He is explicit about the role acting plays in his self-created political theater. In an earlier scene from *3 Henry VI*, incorporated by Olivier into Richard's opening soliloquy in *Richard III*, Richard states, "Why, I can smile, and murder whiles I smile, / ... and wet my cheeks with artificial tears, / And frame my face to all occasions" (3.2.182-5). Because both films grant us an inside view of Richard, we are able to interpret, as many of the characters are not, when he is acting. We recognize, as they cannot, the distance between what he presents as a façade and what he is actually thinking and doing. The effect is to lend a deep irony to the story, as we are privileged with the heavy knowledge that Richard's motivations are always sinister and self-serving.

Richard directs scenes as well as acting in them: One key example of this is the scene in which the townspeople of London come to him and ask him to be king. He presents himself as the devout worshiper, engaged in his daily devotions with two clergy. He resists their invitation to become king, knowing that the more he appears reluctant, the more they will pursue him. With the help of his confidant Buckingham, the entire event is staged as theater and is successful. To the acclaim of the mayor and citizens of London, Richard is hailed as the next King of England.

The conclusion of the story unfolds quickly and almost inevitably. In his ruthless rise to power Richard alienates all of his followers, even loyal Buckingham. They flock to Richmond's faction and help him defeat Richard in battle as Richard calls out in vain: "A horse! A horse! My kingdom for a horse!" Richard's ill-won gains prove to be of less value than a single horse, and his death returns a sense of justice and stability: "the bloody dog is dead." The end of *Richard III* coincides with the end of a century of war and dynastic conflict and with the beginning of the Tudor era, which of course extended, in the person of Queen Elizabeth (Richmond/Henry VII's granddaughter), into Shakespeare's own day.

Despite the sense of poetic justice we are expected to share upon Richard's demise, both film versions of *Richard III* succeed in leaving us haunted by a series of troubling questions. Richard has effectively demonstrated that politics and kingship are matters of performance. His world is a modern world in which image is everything, and the people will believe what they want to believe. Olivier's film creates the lingering impression that perhaps all politics is about appearance rather than reality. His Richard remains a compelling figure even in his excesses. Richard Loncraine's film brings these issues even more explicitly into the frame; his modern setting connects Richard to fascism and suggests that other forms of the cult of personality may be equally successful, especially during times of crisis. The plot's resolution is, on one level, meant to signal a return of peace and stability, but both films leave viewers with a suspicion that Richard may be a Machiavellian prototype, the last of which we have not seen.

Analysis and Interpretation: Richard III

1. Olivier's film adds a number of lines from *3 Henry VI* to Richard's opening soliloquy (see the end of Act 3, scene 2). What do these additional lines reveal about Richard? What do they contribute to our understanding of Richard and his character?

2. Loncraine and McKellen's screenplay cuts about two-thirds of the lines from Shakespeare's play. How do you think they made decisions about what to cut and what to keep? How does such a radical editing of the play work?

3. Why do you think these filmmakers chose *Richard III* to remake as a film? What about the play makes it attractive for reworking in cinematic terms? Why would a film based on this history be attractive to modern audiences?

4. Both Olivier and Loncraine use a variety of film devices to build the audience's relationship with the main character. Besides direct eye contact with the camera, what other techniques do their films use to create an intimate relationship with Richard? Does Richard become a more "sympathetic" character as a result? Why or why not?

5. Olivier's version was filmed almost entirely indoors on small-scale sets at Shepperton Studios in England, with the exception of the late battle scenes, which were filmed outdoors in Spain. How does Olivier use this enclosed set to create mood and tension? Make note of the points at which doorways and windows are used to frame characters or scenes. How do these visual boundaries work to define the story space of the film?

6. Loncraine makes a bold decision to set his film in the 1930s. While the language is still taken directly from Shakespeare's text, the art direction and visual elements create a world that few viewers would recognize as "traditional Shakespeare." What is the effect of this radical chronological shift?

7. Both Olivier and Loncraine use *Richard III* to present a view of politics as stagecraft or illusion. Why does Richard fail, if he is so good at "acting" like a king? Is there evidence in either film that politics is something other than manipulation or theater? How would the "ideal" king rule, if not through the power of rhetoric and political theater?

8. The symbolism of "the crown" is used repeatedly in Olivier's film. How does this visual icon function to suggest some kind of ideal of kingship? What values or power is the crown meant to signify?

Henry V

The opening scenes of *Henry V* raise important questions about the right of one ruler or country to invade another. In the first major action of the play, King Henry consults with his bishops and lords about the legal and moral justification for invading France to assert his claim to the French crown. While the bishops assure Henry that he has both a legal and a moral right to wage war on France for the purpose of claiming the crown, we know from the previous scene that their motivations are in fact self-serving. The entire legal and theological justification for Henry's war on France remains suspect—a diversionary tactic the bishops concoct to keep King Henry distracted from a pending bill that would strip the church of much of its lands and wealth.

Nonetheless, Henry's French campaign ends in his success, both in war and in love. Outnumbered significantly, his army wins a resounding and improbable victory on the field at Agincourt. To cement the new English-French monarchy, at the end of the play Henry has succeeded in winning the hand of Katharine, daughter of France's Charles VI. The play ends as preparations are being made for their wedding. The closing lines of the play, spoken by the Chorus, describe King Henry as the "star of England." *Henry V* ends at the very pinnacle of success, but the Chorus reminds us the triumph will be short-lived. Upon Henry's death, his son is "in infant bands crowned King," and the audience would have known

79

of the return of war and the loss of France under Henry VI that is soon to come.

If Richard III serves as the model villain in Shakespeare's histories, Henry V stands in marked contrast as the model King. The preceding plays, the first and second parts of *Henry IV*, have chronicled his youth, notoriously misspent in the company of Falstaff, drinking and clubbing and womanizing. Yet it turns out that Prince Hal's youthful excesses have humanized him and made him a more well-rounded, compassionate ruler as he becomes King Henry. He is able to relate to and understand the common people, as his speeches to his troops on the eve of battle amply demonstrate. While "the courses of his youth promised it not" (1.1.25), Henry has matured and grown into the role of king in a remarkable fashion:

> The breath no sooner left his father's body
> But that his wildness, mortified in him,
> Seemed to die too; yea, at that very moment
> Consideration like an angel came
> And whipped th' offending Adam out of him,
> Leaving his body as a paradise
> T' envelop and contain celestial spirits. (1.1.26-32)

In this sudden transformation, Hal's wildness is remade by consideration; the star of England is figured forth from out of the pubs and brothels of his wild and misspent youth.

Henry V
Laurence Olivier, Director, 1944

Felix Aylmer— *Archbishop of Canterbury*	Morland Graham— *Sir Thomas Erpingham*
Leslie Banks—*Chorus*	Laurence Olivier— *King Henry V*
Robert Helpmann— *Bishop of Ely*	

Henry V
Kenneth Branagh, Director, 1989

Derek Jacobi—*Chorus*

Kenneth Branagh—*Henry V*

Simon Shepherd—*Gloucester*

James Larkin—*Bedford*

Brian Blessed—*Exeter*

James Simmons—*York*

Charles Kay—*Canterbury*

Alec McCowen—*Ely*

Fabian Cartwright—*Cambridge*

Stephen Simms—*Scroop*

Jay Villers—*Grey Edward*

Jewesbury—*Erpingham*

Ian Holm—*Fluellen*

Two feature films present quite different visions of Henry as king. Laurence Olivier's 1944 film works hard to present a patriotic, gleaming image for the king. Olivier simply omits some of the scenes that show a darker side, choosing instead to create a film that presents the star of England in colorful and unmediated glory. Kenneth Branagh's 1989 film offers a powerful and dark contrast. We do see the violent and extreme side of political authority; the battle scenes are dark, muddy, and realistic. Branagh's Henry must execute friends and threaten vengeful violence upon the people of the city of Harfleur. His Henry undoubtedly knows some of what Richard III knows about the contingencies of politics as theater. Branagh's Henry seems, at least on the surface, much more in keeping with a skeptical modern view of political authority.

The visual styles of the two films also stand in marked contrast to one another. This contrast is quite visible in the color images printed in the Bevington anthology. Plate 14 shows Laurence Olivier as Henry V, on board a ship en route to France. The colors are bright and sunny, and the patriotic overtones are apparent in the King's posture. Plate 17 shows Kenneth Branagh as King Henry, on a muddy battlefield following his victory at Agincourt. His weariness even in victory and the bloody corpses stacked in the wagon he speaks from paint a different picture of war than what we see in the Olivier film.

Olivier's film begins (as we saw in chapter 1) with a historical re-enactment of The Globe theater and the play as it might have been performed in 1600. His sets are two-dimensional, painterly, and evoke a medieval book of hours. The film has the look of a children's puppet show rather than a realistic military drama. Branagh also employs elaborate framing devices and the figure of the Chorus to mediate between us and the events of the film, but its look and style are more gritty and realistic. Is Shakespeare's Henry the glorious hero we see in Olivier's film? Or is he the dark and brooding figure of Branagh's remake? As usual, Shakespeare provides ample textual support for both views. The subtlety of *Henry V* is that we see him as both a hero and a Machiavellian manipulator. The resulting vision of kingship and power is remarkably ambivalent and modern, which is certainly a part of the reason the play works so successfully on-screen for contemporary audiences.

Analysis and Interpretation: Henry V

1. How does Olivier use the figure of the Chorus and the framing of The Globe theater's stage to frame the events of his film? What is the function of the Chorus in the film?

2. Branagh uses the prologue and the Chorus to call our attention to the fact that we are watching a film, a constructed visual representation. What effect does this device have on our responses to the events?

3. Make a list of important scenes from the play not included in Olivier's film. How many of these scenes are included in Branagh's version of the film? How do these scenes change the picture of King Henry that we see?

4. The Criterion DVD version of the Olivier *Henry V* includes a series of images taken from a medieval book of hours. If you have access to this DVD, explore these images and think about their use as a model for the style of Olivier's film. The use of a two-dimensional painterly style is important in several scenes in the film. Which scenes most evidently rely on this style?

What contrasting styles are used in other scenes? Is there a pattern to the way contrasting visual styles are used in the film?

5. How does Branagh's Chorus work to remind viewers of the artificiality of film as a medium? Does the Chorus's appearance on the battlefield affect your relationship to the events of the film? How? Why would Branagh want to use the Chorus in this manner?

6. Olivier's film of *Henry V* has occasionally been criticized as a piece of wartime propaganda. Do you agree with this criticism? What evidence from the film complicates or challenges this critique?

7. Is Branagh's *Henry V*, as some viewers have suggested, more realistic or critical in its depiction of the king and his power? In what ways does the film present King Henry as a myth or hero? In what ways does it present him "realistically"? Can it do both?

A Chronology of Shakespeare's History Plays

	Play	Date Written	Dates and Events Covered
The "second tetralogy" (textual evidence suggests these plays were written later than the plays of the "first tetralogy")	*Richard II*	1595	(1398-1399) Struggle between King Richard II and Henry Bolingbroke (later King Henry IV); deposition and murder of Richard II
	1 Henry IV	1596-97	(1402-1403) Uprisings in Scotland and Wales; battle of Shrewsbury, at which Prince Hal kills Harry Percy (Hotspur)
	2 Henry IV	1597	(1403-1413) From the aftermath of the Battle of Shrewsbury to the death of King Henry IV
	*Henry V**	1599	(1415) Henry V's campaign in France; siege of Harfleur, military victory over French at Agincourt; plans for marriage to Katherine of Valois (to cement link to French crown)

"The first tetralogy" (textual evidence suggests these plays were written prior to the plays of the "second tetralogy")	1 Henry VI	c. 1589-92	(1422-1453) From the funeral of Henry V to the death of John Talbot, Earl of Shrewsbury. Henry accepts Margaret of Anjou as his queen.
	2 Henry VI	c. 1589-92	(1445-1455) Marriage of Henry and Margaret; loss of French lands; up to first battle of St Alban's
	3 Henry VI	c. 1589-92	(1460-1471) The military phase of the Wars; from the aftermath of the first battle of St Alban's to the defeat of Queen Margaret at Tewksbury.
	Richard III*	c. 1591-94	(1471-1485) Death of King Edward IV; Richard Gloucester's rise to the Protectorship and his ruthless rise to the throne; Richmond defeats Richard at the battle of Bosworth and is crowned King Henry VII (the first Tudor king).

*Films based on *Henry V* and *Richard III* are discussed in Chapter 3.

CHAPTER 4

The Tragedies

The video for Kenneth Branagh's *Hamlet* (1996) includes a short special feature on the making of the film, in which Robin Williams and Billy Crystal (each has a small part in the film) imagine William Shakespeare trying to pitch *Hamlet* to a present-day film-industry executive. Playing the part of a cynical studio executive, Robin Williams says: "We're really excited. The whole first half is *just great*. Can we lose the ghost? It's just a lot of negativity. And that whole death thing—we'd like it at the end if *he* lives." And here's Billy Crystal's rendition of the executive producer's reply to Shakespeare: "Sorry, Bill. We're crazy about you here, we are; the hair, the beard, the whole thing. But it's just *too much of a downer*. Isn't there anything for Jim Carrey to do in this?" With their characteristic humor and wit, the two comic actors point to the difficulties inherent in filming the tragedies for modern audiences. Modern film audiences often want entertainment and escape, not *tragedy*; so filmmakers have to find ways to reimagine tragedy, in the visual medium of film, for audiences who may not be familiar with the plots of Shakespeare's great tragic works.

Fortunately for us, filmmakers have been both prolific and inventive in their approaches to the tragedies. The tragedies have been produced on film by some of our greatest directors and actors, in a variety of different adaptations and styles. From Laurence Olivier's black-and-white 1948 psychological exploration of *Hamlet* to Baz Luhrmann's edgy, postmodern re-interpretation of *Romeo and Juliet* (1996), filmed versions of the tragedies offer a wider and more ambitious range of film texts to be explored than any other genre. This chapter focuses on *Romeo and Juliet*, *Hamlet*, and *Othello*. Additional films based on *Macbeth* and *King Lear* are also addressed in chapter 5.

Tragic Form and Structure

What makes a tragedy tragic? How are tragedies supposed to make us feel? What's the difference between a story that is simply "a downer," as Billy Crystal's imaginary film producer might say, and one that is "tragic" in a Shakespearean sense? Shakespeare himself never wrote any criticism or theory which would help us to understand his ideas about tragic drama and its function, so we have to look elsewhere. As it turns out, a large body of critical work has been devoted to tragedy, extending as far back as classical antiquity, to the time of the great Athenian dramas of Aeschylus, Sophocles, and Euripides.

For the Greeks, at least as we understand them through the writings of Aristotle, tragic drama served important social functions. Tragedy, for them, was not just about death and violence, nor was it supposed to be sentimental or maudlin. Instead, tragedy involved what Aristotle called *catharsis*, the process of purging emotions by arousing them. Specifically, Aristotle argued that tragedy works to purge audiences of pity and fear through the process of catharsis. If tragic characters is are good people who suffer bad fortune by chance or accident, we may feel pity for their bad luck, but we'll also feel that their downfall was random and unjust. In contrast, if the tragic characters are simply evil, we may feel that justice is served in their downfall, but we won't feel much empathy for them. For the tragic catharsis to do its work on us, we need to feel both things at once. The tragic characters need to be good enough that we feel a sense of loss or pity at their bad fortunes, yet morally suspect enough so that we also feel that, at least in part, they got what was coming to them.

The lasting appeal of Shakespeare's tragedies on film suggests that his characters continue to offer this kind of complexity and balance for modern audiences. The great tragic figures like Hamlet still work for us because we can see enough of ourselves in them that we do feel connected to them, because we are like them; yet they are also responsible for or complicit in their own downfalls, so we understand their ends as at least partially just or deserved.

Comedy, as we saw in chapter 2, generally moves from one kind of society to another, with a new society forming around the main characters at the end. Tragedy often disrupts the social order and leaves it fragmented. Tragic characters raise questions that undermine faith in the order of things; they set in motion powerful disruptive forces that tear their society apart. Comic endings tend to reassure audiences that things are repaired and restored, and that the central conflicts explored in the main action of the play have been resolved. Tragedy, more or less by definition, has a contrasting dynamic, and tragic plots leave audiences feeling unsettled. Tragedies often end with the death or exile of their main characters, but, even in death, the tragic heroes usually leave in their wake deep concerns about the spiritual and political health of the world they have inhabited.

Where comedy is, in Frye's view, the mythos of spring, a time of rebirth and renewal, tragedy is the mythos of autumn, a more philosophical season of decline and fall. For Frye, as for Aristotle, tragedy focuses on a central character who is somewhat elevated above the "average" members of his or her society and yet below the level of a god. In a rather elegant metaphor, Frye writes, "tragic heroes are so much the highest points in their human landscape that they seem the inevitable conductors of the power about them, great trees more likely to be struck by lightning than a clump of grass" (*Anatomy of Criticism*, 207).

At the same time, however, it is important that tragic characters also have a human side that allows audiences to identify with them. Unlike gods or the characters of myth or epic, tragic heroes are subject to more or less the same laws of nature and causality as we are. They are not magical or superhuman, and they cannot escape the consequences of their own actions. As Frye puts it, "However thickly strewn a tragedy may be with ghosts, portents, witches, or oracles, we know that the tragic hero cannot simply rub a lamp and summon a genie to get him out of his trouble" (207).

Many of Shakespeare's tragic characters would seem to fit Frye's model. Think of Othello, for example; once he begins to follow the insidious logic of jealousy and mistrust planted in his mind by Iago, he seems unable to reverse its course, becoming caught up in the vortex of violence he himself has unleashed. Macbeth, too, once he starts the tragic consequences in motion with the murder of Duncan, is unable to stop their murderous course until he becomes a victim. Even Hamlet, perhaps the most complex tragic hero in Shakespeare, is overwhelmed with the secret knowledge (given him by his father's ghost) that his father has been murdered by his uncle, Claudius. Frye offers an especially useful formulation of the double-bind in which the tragic hero finds himself: "The tragic hero is very great as compared with us, but there is something else, something on the side of him opposite the audience, compared to which he is small. This something else may be called God, gods, fate, accident, fortune, necessity, circumstance, or any combination of these, but whatever it is the tragic hero is our mediator with it" (207).

As this process works itself out in tragic drama, the plot dynamic typically works to move toward some kind of recognition, awareness, or truth. Aristotle described this tragic recognition as "a change from ignorance to knowledge" and Frye called it an "epiphany of law, of that which is and must be" (208). Frye's view is that, for Shakespeare, this law is connected to Renaissance science and its emerging view of nature: "The tragic process in Shakespeare is natural in the sense that it simply happens, whatever its cause, explanation, or relationships. Characters may grope about for conceptions of gods that kill us for their sport, or for a divinity that shapes our ends, but the action of tragedy will not abide our questions" (208).

Shakespearean tragedy maintains a delicate balance between fatalism and moralism. As much as we might feel like a particular character is simply acting out a preordained fate, we also need to feel that he or she is making choices or taking actions that shape the outcome. The plays would not be especially moving or interesting if it we simply felt that the characters were victims of bad luck or fate. Conversely, we also need to feel that the tragic characters are not simply getting their due for breaking some kind of moral code. Macbeth may be a murderer, but his story is not simply about revenge or poetic justice. Shakespeare usually surrounds his tragic characters with other characters who interpret, comment, and analyze what is happening, but somehow we always know that none of these interpretations quite give us the whole story. Shakespeare's tragedies are different from more fatalistic classical Greek dramas, and they're also a step or two away from modern existentialism. Multiple interpretations are almost always presented within the plays themselves, and this lends the tragedies a great deal of depth and complexity as subjects for films.

Preview Questions: Tragic Form and Structure

1. Look at the main character in one of the tragedies. How does this character compare to other characters in the play? What are his or her attributes, qualities, talents, or characteristics? What elevates this character above the norms of society?

2. What forces or events in the play seem to have power over (or greater than) the main character? What drives or motivates the main character? Are there any supernatural or nonhuman forces in the play (ghosts, gods, prophets, "destiny")? On what authority do these nonhuman characters speak? How do they influence the thoughts and actions of the human characters?

3. Look for characters in the play who comment on the actions. (For example, Polonius, who interprets Hamlet's behavior as evidence that he is lovesick for Ophelia.) What interpretation do these characters offer? How convincing are their comments or analyses?

4. Find the key moments of recognition and/or reversal in the plot. At what point does the direction of the plot shift or change? Why? Is there a clearly identifiable "moment of truth" or recognition? What is recognized? By whom?

5. Instead of looking for a single "tragic flaw," list as many possible traits or motivations that might *possibly* account for a tragic character's actions or thoughts. How many of these interpretations are supported by the evidence in the play? Why?

6. Do any of Shakespeare's *female* characters fit Northrop Frye's model of the tragic hero? (Lady Macbeth? Ophelia? Cordelia?) How might a feminist theory of tragedy rewrite both Frye and Aristotle? Which characters in which plays would you begin with in order to build a feminist theory of tragedy? Why?

The Tragedies on Film

Unlike the comedies, which focus on groups of characters, many of whom are stock types rather than developed characters, Shakespeare's tragedies generally focus on central figures who are deep, complex, analytical, and astute commentators on their experiences. Further, the plots of the major tragedies are open to multiple angles of interpretation and they tend to leave things open-ended and unresolved, unlike the comedies, which almost always tie things up neatly at the end. For these reasons and others, the tragedies have received substantially more attention from filmmakers over the years than have the comedies. *Hamlet* has been the favorite subject for filmed treatments. Among the other major tragedies, *Romeo and Juliet* and *Othello* have drawn the attention of some of the film industry's best and brightest. Consequently, we have multiple film versions of each of these plays, making it possible to use a comparative strategy to further develop our critical analyses.

Romeo and Juliet

As David Bevington suggests, *Romeo and Juliet* is a tragedy with a dual focus, one on the star-crossed young lovers and a second on their families, whose "ancient grudge" boils over into "new mutiny" and brings grief to the people of Verona. "The city itself is a kind of protagonist, suffering through its own violence and coming at last to the sad comfort that wisdom brings" (1008). The tragedy comes with the lesson that only through the death of the lovers can that sad wisdom be purchased. This tragic recognition comes to the Capulet and Montague households as the Friar retells the story of Romeo and Juliet's "misadventured, piteous overthrows" and they realize, too late, their own complicity in the deaths of their children.

Romeo and Juliet does not precisely fit the classical Aristotelian definition of tragedy outlined above. As tragic protagonists, Romeo and Juliet lack stature and depth; they are very young (in their early teens), typical teenagers in many ways, with the exception of their passionate attachment to one another. The major obstacle to their love comes from their parents and is characteristic of the domestic comedies of Shakespeare's early career more than the tragedies of his later phases. The tragic recognition so important in Aristotle's view of tragedy is not something they experience themselves, because they are already dead by the time it happens. The recognition comes instead to their parents, and by extension to the community of Verona as a whole, when it becomes clear that the young lovers are dead as a result of a continuing cycle of violence and revenge that encompasses the city.

Like many of the comedies (but few of the tragedies), Romeo and Juliet ends with the restoration of order. Capulet and Montague, grieving for the loss of their children, at last bury their strife with a ceremonial handshake in the public scene that closes the play, in a mood described by the Chorus as "a gloomy peace." The play shares both comic and tragic elements. The theme of young love suddenly flowering despite parental opposition links it to comedies like A Midsummer Night's Dream, while the tragic cycle of violence that exacts the price of the young couple's death renders the comic elements tragic with a poignant and bittersweet overtone. This is not the dark tragedy of Othello, but the exquisite agony of youthful passion, the flame that burns so bright only because it fades so fast.

The Chorus who opens the play tells us how things are going to end and, by doing so, adds an aura of inevitability to the plot. From the beginning, the lovers are identified as "star-crossed" and we are told that "with their death" they will "bury their parents' strife." Is their death inevitable? What does it mean that they are "star-crossed"? "The concept is deliberately broad," Bevington explains, "encompassing many factors, such as hatred, bumbling, bad luck, and simple lack of awareness" (1006). As with many of the tragedies, there is a balance between fate and human agency in *Romeo and Juliet*. Structurally, the play suggests the feud between the Montagues and Capulets as a primary cause of the tragedy: The first scene is a street fight, and the Chorus suggests family enmity as the main reason for the lovers' deaths. Yet both chance and human actions play a part in the outcome as well. Letters are not delivered in time; Romeo rashly chooses to duel with Tybalt even though he knows he is risking death or banishment.

Two major films have been made of *Romeo and Juliet*, each making a serious effort to make the story speak to a new generation of young people. Franco Zeffirelli's 1968 film was self-consciously crafted to appeal to the youth culture of the 1960s. Baz Luhrmann's 1996 film, *William Shakespeare's Romeo + Juliet* brought a postmodern sensibility and a frenetic visual style to the media-savvy youth of the 1990s.

Romeo and Juliet
Franco Zeffirelli, Director, 1968

Leonard Whiting—*Romeo*

Olivia Hussey—*Juliet*

John McEnery—*Mercutio*

Michael York—*Tybalt*

Milo O'Shea—*Friar Laurence*

Pat Heywood—*The Nurse*

Paul Hardwick—*Lord Capulet*

Natasha Parry—*Lady Capulet*

Antonio Pierfederici—*Lord Montague*

Esmerelda Ruspoli—*Lady Montague*

Keith Skinner—*Balthazar*

Franco Zeffirelli's film of *Romeo and Juliet* originally played in 1968, during the Vietnam war, at a time when the emergent youth culture of the 1960s was articulating an ethos of passion, love, and peace against an older generation's conservatism and militarism. The cultural conflicts in the air at that time coincided with the theme of generational conflict in Shakespeare's text, and Zeffirelli's film highlighted these connections. Zeffirelli chose to use actors (Leonard Whiting and Olivia Hussey) who were young and relatively unknown, so audiences would be able to see them as the teenage lovers with little or no interference. This strategy was almost the direct opposite of his decision to cast Elizabeth Taylor and Richard Burton in his 1966 *Taming of the Shrew* (see chapter 2). Where the audience for *Taming* would see Taylor and Burton first and Kate and Petruchio second, audiences for *Romeo and Juliet* would see not the actors, but the characters.

Zeffirelli's film is visually stunning. It was filmed in coastal Italian towns that look like realistic versions of fifteenth-century Verona. The costumes and sets are lush, detailed, and authentic, and the film won Academy Awards for cinematography and costumes. As one critic writes, Zeffirelli's film successfully presents "a solid and believable world of dimension and substance" (Welsh 82). The film opens with a sweeping high shot overlooking "Verona" that visually echoes the opening sequence of Laurence Olivier's 1944 *Henry V* (see chapter 1). In *Romeo and Juliet*, it is in fact the voice of Olivier himself that delivers the opening Chorus as a voice-over as the camera pans across the cityscape. As the camera descends into the city, we find ourselves in a crowded, bustling, dusty marketplace, replete with onions and peppers ripening on vendors' wagons. The Capulet boys appear in bright red and yellow velvet suits; the Montagues follow soon afterward in dark greens and blues. The costumes lend even the fight scenes a feeling of summer warmth and sensuality. Zeffirelli's visual style in the film might be called heightened realism. The settings are believable and the costuming and locations are all historically authentic and believable. The result is to translate the play fully into a cinematic mode and style.

Zeffirelli presents Shakespeare's play as an actual event unfolding before our eyes rather than as a staged drama.

Zeffirelli's desire to bring a new audience to the play may have contributed to his streamlined script. Only about one third of the play's text remains, and many of Zeffirelli's cuts work to create more simplified and one-dimensional versions of the lead characters. Zeffirelli's Romeo and Juliet are less reflective and philosophical than Shakespeare's, but they appeared to resonate nonetheless for the youthful film audiences of 1968, who made the film one of the most popular and successful Shakespeare-based films of all time.

Analysis and Interpretation

1. How does Zeffirelli present the relationship between Romeo and Juliet? What kind of body language and nonverbal cues does he use to suggest the nature of their relationship? How does his screenplay edit and reshape their lines to present them to a film audience?

2. Does Zeffirelli's film suggest that fate plays a role in the lovers' deaths? To what extent are the lovers shown in his version to be part of a larger process or cycle of violence? How is their tragedy explained or understood by the characters around them? What other explanations for the tragedy does the film offer? How much does chance play a role? Do any of the characters exhibit any "tragic flaws"? How is this shown in the film?

3. Many critics have seen in this film echoes of the "generation gap" characteristic of popular culture in the 1960s. What evidence do you see of this in the film? What kind of social commentary do you think Zeffirelli is offering through his choice of Shakespeare's tragedy of love? What choices does Zeffirelli make as a director to reinforce his views?

4. How does Zeffirelli's film present the Montague and Capulet parents? Are they effective role models? What are their own marriages like? What role do they play in the film and its

outcomes? What kind of spin is put on them as parents and role models?

5. By presenting a more accessible and streamlined version of Shakespeare, has Zeffirelli "gone too far" in his efforts to popularize the play for a 1960s audience? What is lost in his translation to the medium of film? What is gained by his editing and visual style?

William Shakespeare's Romeo + Juliet
Baz Luhrmann, Director, 1996

Leonardo DiCaprio—*Romeo*	Diane Venora—*Gloria Capulet*
Claire Danes—*Juliet*	
Edwina Moore—*Anchorwoman (Chorus)*	Brian Dennehy—*Ted Montague*
John Leguizamo—*Tybalt*	Christina Pickles—*Caroline Montague*
Harold Perrineau, Jr.—*Mercutio*	Vondie Curtis-Hall—*Captain Prince*
Paul Sorvino—*Fulgencio Capulet*	Paul Rudd—*Dave Paris*

A quick look at the names of some of the characters listed in the cast list (above) for Baz Luhrmann's 1996 version of *Romeo and Juliet* suggests the way Luhrmann has updated the play for a new youth-culture audience. Lord Montague has become "Ted," and the Chorus is now identified as a TV "Anchorwoman." Like Franco Zeffirelli in the 1960s, Luhrmann has devised a filmmaking strategy based on an explicit desire to merge Shakespeare's play with contemporary youth culture. Luhrmann sets his film in the present, in a world populated with gun-toting gangs and heavily armed police helicopters patrolling the lawless streets. Luhrmann's editing is fast-paced, and the visual style of the film is vibrant, excessive, and replete with both pop culture icons and religious symbols.

With John Leguizamo as Tybalt, in a setting that evokes a combination of Miami, Los Angeles, and Rio, the film has a distinctively Latin as opposed to Italian flavor. The Latin Capulets are countered by the Anglo Montagues, with African Americans cast in mediating roles (Mercutio and Captain Prince, most notably), so that the issue of race and ethnicity is layered onto the family conflicts present in Shakespeare's play. We cannot help but see allegorical layers of meaning in the film as an indirect but effective commentary on gang violence and racial conflict.

Shakespeare's Verona has become Luhrmann's Verona Beach, a sultry city at once opulent and run-down. Here is the way one setting, a downtrodden beach-front amusement park, is described by Luhrmann and his coauthor Craig Pearce in the screenplay:

EXT. BEACH. DAWN.
To the melancholic strains of Mozart's "Serenade for Winds," we discover the ornate arch of what is left of a once splendid cinema. At the top of the arch the words "Sycamore Grove" are clearly visible. The cinema has been demolished but for its proscenium, through which we can see the grubby shore of Verona Beach, housing a collection of sex clubs and strip joints, populated with prostitutes, drag queens, clients, and street people. (17)

Towering over this street scene are three symbolic structures that function as icons throughout the film. Two high-rise chrome and steel buildings loom above opposite ends of the street, each adorned with a huge lighted sign, one reading Montague, the other Capulet. The two rival families are refigured in Luhrmann's film as mega-corporations, dominating the landscape of Verona Beach much as they dominate its economy. The third symbol is religious, a giant statue of Jesus that looks very much like the famous real-life statue of Christ, arms outspread, overlooking the city of Rio de Janeiro, Brazil. The camera returns to this statue repeatedly throughout the film, and religions icons appear in many other scenes as well, from a church filled with blue neon crosses at Juliet's funeral to the tiny cross she wears around her neck.

In the preface to the screenplay, Luhrmann writes: "We're trying to make this movie rambunctious, sexy, violent, and entertaining in the way Shakespeare might have if he had been a filmmaker. We have not shied away from clashing low comedy with high tragedy, which is the style of the play, for it's the low comedy that allows you to embrace the very high emotions of the tragedy" (vi). Luhrmann retains Shakespeare's original language, however, in doing so; this is not *West Side Story*, but still recognizable as *Romeo and Juliet* "in the original language," even if transplanted to a contemporary setting. Baz Luhrmann's intentions are clear enough: his goal is to (re-)create a Shakespeare for the masses, a modern film tragedy that a wide range of audiences can understand and enjoy, and yet to do so in the language of Shakespeare.

Analysis and Interpretation

1. Baz Luhrmann chooses to update the setting of *Romeo and Juliet* to the present day and yet at the same time to retain Shakespeare's language. What effect does the Shakespearean language and stylized dialogue have on the film? How would the film be different if the language were updated to contemporary English?

2. Keep track of the religious iconography and symbolism used throughout the film. What is its function? Is this a religious film? Do you think the religious imagery heightens or emphasizes a religious theme? Why or why not?

3. Look carefully at the ending of Luhrmann's film. How is it different from Shakespeare's? What effect do these differences have on the tone of the film?

4. Luhrmann uses the framing device of television news coverage as a way of revising the Chorus in a contemporary context. One reviewer has suggested that this makes his film "darker" than Zeffirelli's, because Romeo and Juliet become just another news story—another tragedy getting its fifteen minutes of fame, only to be forgotten. Do you agree with this

interpretation? How do you think the news story framework functions in the film?

5. Make a log of the different camera angles and shots used in Luhrmann's film. Notice the diverse range of shots used, from high overhead (helicopter views) to extreme close-ups. The camera seems to move in and out of the scenes from many angles and directions. Where are we positioned as viewers by Luhrmann's camera and editing? Are we encouraged to share the world of the two lovers? Are we outside looking in? Or something else? How does Luhrmann use the camera to create and establish our relationship to the actors? To the story?

6. Is there any change in the pacing and style of the shots when the camera is focused on the two young lovers? How does the film create a sense of intimacy with and closeness to these characters?

7. Is Luhrmann's film still "tragedy" in the sense Shakespeare might have understood? Has the story become something else entirely in its new setting and visual style? What is "tragic" about Luhrmann's film? How is his sense of tragedy similar to and different from Shakespeare's? How does Luhrmann's sense of tragedy compare to Zeffirelli's?

Hamlet

If the substantial history of *Hamlet* on film is any indication, Shakespeare's most famous tragedy is something of a Rorschach test for directors. *Hamlet* is like an inkblot on a page, and interpreting the blot says more about the interpreter than it does about the inkblot. Laurence Olivier's 1948 *Hamlet*, for example, has been seen as the most "Freudian" and psychological interpretation of the play. Kenneth Branagh's 1996 version is the most obsessive and perfectionistic, keeping virtually every line of the original play intact and in order, to deliver a 242-minute epic version of Shakespeare's longest play. Branagh's *Hamlet* is, as a result, the most political of the filmed versions. Interpreting Hamlet (the character and the play) seems to be something filmmakers love and need to do, and they end up providing readers of the play with a stunning array of different visual narratives to add to the existing storehouse of critical knowledge about the great tragedy. The filmmakers also reveal a good bit about themselves and their own interpretations of the play along the way. Many of Shakespeare's tragedies can be interpreted in multiple ways, but none more so than *Hamlet*, and the diverse range of different film treatments bears ample witness to this fact. We'll focus here on the four most widely available and widely different feature film versions: Olivier's, Franco Zeffirelli's (starring Mel Gibson in 1990), Branagh's, and Michael Almereyda's (set in contemporary Manhattan, starring Ethan Hawke).

Hamlet
Laurence Olivier, Director, 1948

Laurence Olivier—*Hamlet*	Peter Cushing—*Osric*
Basil Sydney—*Claudius*	Anthony Quayle—*Marcellus*
Eileen Herlie—*Gertrude*	Edmond Knight—*Barnardo*
Jean Simmons—*Ophelia*	John Laurie—*Francisco*
Felix Aylmer—*Polonius*	Stanley Holloway—
Terence Morgan—*Laertes*	*Gravedigger*
Norman Woodland—*Horatio*	

Laurence Olivier's 1948 black-and-white *Hamlet* may well stand as the most influential Shakespeare film ever, as well as the most influential interpretation of the play. The entire film seems to be shrouded in fog and deep shadows; Olivier's Castle Elsinore is mazelike, stony, and cold, establishing an atmosphere of alienation, isolation, and despair. The visual style of Olivier's film owes much to the *film noir* genre. *Film noir* was a visual mode or genre, popular in the late 1940s and early 1950s, made famous in films like *The Maltese Falcon* and Orson Welles's *Touch of Evil*. *Film noir* usually involves a detective story or a mystery, a narrative suffused with an aura of corruption and suspicion. In a *film noir*, nothing is what is appears to be, and usually every character in the story turns out to be corrupt and disingenuous. The *film noir* ethos works in Olivier's film to highlight the corruption of the Danish court and at the same time to contribute to the atmosphere of mystery, intrigue, and surveillance in the play.

Olivier's film establishes a strong interpretation of the play from the very beginning. The film opens with the following lines printed on the screen, appearing before us as Olivier reads them to us in a voice-over:

> So, oft it chances in particular men,
> That for some vicious mole of nature in them,
> By their o'ergrowth of some complexion,
> Oft breaking down the pales and forts of reason,
> Or by some habit grown too much; that these men—
> Carrying, I say, the stamp of one defect,
> Their virtues else, be they as pure as grace,
> Shall in the general censure take corruption
> From that particular fault.

Olivier's opening voice-over monologue concludes with the following statement: "This is the tragedy of a man who could not make up his mind." Thie line is of course Olivier's and not Shakespeare's, and, coupled with the opening speech quoted above, it establishes a firm interpretive framework for the play. The lines above are taken from Act 1, Scene 4, the scene in which Hamlet is commenting on the drinking and revelry of the new King Claudius and his court. Taken out of context and used at the beginning of the film, the lines appear to describe Hamlet himself. Compare Olivier's edited version of the soliloquy to the original text (1.4. 23-36) to see how Olivier's cuts also shift the meaning of the passage.

As David Bevington points out in his introduction, the interpretation of *Hamlet* as a play about indecision or inaction is only partially correct. It's possible to read Hamlet's delay and patience as a calculating and indeed effective strategy rather than as a central tragic flaw in his character. Nonetheless, Olivier's reading of the play as presented in this film has surely influenced generations of filmmakers and probably some teachers and students of *Hamlet* as well. Olivier's screenplay cuts just over half of the text, and omits several characters, including Rosencrantz and Guildenstern. The entire Fortinbras subplot is also cut from Olivier's film, erasing a significant political subtext.

Olivier himself described his film as an "essay in Hamlet" and not as a film version of the play. He wrote: "I feel it is misleading to couple Shakespeare's play with the film of 'Hamlet,' and for this reason. In Shakespeare's play, as in all his plays, there runs a beautifully intricate and complete pattern of character and action. The only satisfactory way of appreciating all that Shakespeare meant by 'Hamlet' is to sit down in a theater and follow a performance of the great play in its entirety" (Behrens and Rosen, 748). Despite this disclaimer, it's still very interesting to look at Olivier's film in the context of the play's text, to see what the great actor and filmmaker chose to dwell on in his presentation of the tragedy.

Analysis and Interpretation

1. Olivier made a conscious choice to film his *Hamlet* in black and white. He wanted the whole film to be in muted tones (in stark contrast to his extremely colorful *Henry V*, filmed four years earlier, in 1944; see chapter 3). How do you think the black-and-white photography contributes to the emotional effect of the film? How would it be different if filmed in color?

2. Olivier used a number of camera techniques to represent his idea of *Hamlet* visually. There are many deep focus shots, where both foreground and background are in visible focus. There are moments (when Hamlet sees the ghost of his father, for example) when the camera blurs in and out of focus to the rhythm of a beating heart. In other scenes, the camera hovers high above the actors on the set. Olivier also used numerous doorways and archways to visually frame and separate the actors in given scenes. Watch carefully for these and other camera techniques and make a list of distinctive shots. How do these shots affect the look and effect of given moments in the film?

3. How does Olivier's decision to focus on *Hamlet* as a psychological drama affect your understanding of the play? What does he show about Hamlet's character, motivation, or makeup that helps you to understand him better? How do you understand Olivier's interpretation of the play as "the tragedy of a man who could not make up his mind"? What does this help illustrate about the play? What does it distort or leave out?

4. Do some background reading to learn more about *film noir*. How does Olivier's film exhibit some of the visual and narrative characteristics of the genre? Critics have also noted the use of "expressionistic" techniques. What is German expressionism in film? How does Olivier's film exemplify expressionist techniques and strategies?

Hamlet
Franco Zeffirelli, Director, 1990

Mel Gibson—*Hamlet*	Paul Scofield—*Ghost*
Alan Bates—*Claudius*	Michael Maloney—
Glenn Close—*Gertrude*	*Rosencrantz*
Helena Bonham Carter—	Sean Murray—*Guildenstern*
Ophelia	Trevor Peacock—
Nathaniel Parker—*Laertes*	*Gravedigger*
Stephen Dillane—*Horatio*	John McEnery—*Osric*
Ian Holm—*Polonius*	

Olivier's 1948 *Hamlet* so dominated the cinematic landscape that it was over forty years before another feature film was made of the play. Franco Zeffirelli's decision to cast action-hero Mel Gibson in the lead raised some eyebrows, to say the least, but the film was considered to be a reasonable success on both the critical and the financial fronts after all. As he did with *Romeo and Juliet*, Zeffirelli creates with his *Hamlet* a visual feast, with detailed costumes and wonderful set design. His Elsinore is almost medieval, more primitive, dusty, and earthy than Olivier's (and certainly a stark contrast to Branagh's use of the opulent Blenheim Palace for his Elsinore). Casting Gibson and Glenn Close (as Gertrude) certainly attracted audiences to the theater who may not otherwise have gone to see a Shakespeare film. Zeffirelli's film can be viewed as an effective attempt to produce a relatively accessible and popular film of *Hamlet*. Gibson's Hamlet may not offer the psychological depth and introspection of Olivier's, but it may well be the case that his performance is more understandable and perhaps equally moving for many filmgoers.

In an interview, Franco Zeffirelli confessed that one reason he wanted to cast Gibson as Hamlet was his voice—"I was madly in love with his voice" (Behrens 763). Indeed, Zeffirelli admits that voice and language are the most important and difficult aspects in filming Shakespeare, and his hope is that "in making it [a soliloquy] clear to himself, Mel helps others to understand it better" (764). Gibson's Australian accent does make for good listening, and you may feel more compassion and understanding for his Hamlet than for Olivier's more stagy and theatrical presentation.

Zeffirelli also said some interesting things about his use of color and its relationship to the setting and themes of *Hamlet*. "I keyed the whole movie to mostly grays and ash colors, a 'medieval-primitive' look, the look of a society that is brutal and made of stone. Whenever a few rich colors do come out, the effect is even more vivid. In that sense, this is one of the most colorful films I've ever done—but only because the few rich colors stand out so much from the grays" (764). Zeffirelli's visual style in some ways echoes Olivier's and in other ways departs from it, and the effect of his use of color is indeed striking.

In stark contrast to Olivier's use of *film noir* convention and strategies, Zeffirelli draws instead on action-adventure conventions and styles. The choice of Mel Gibson for the lead role clearly reinforces this genre distinction (it would be impossible for audiences *not* to think of *Mad Max* and *Lethal Weapon* when they looked at Gibson as the Danish prince), as do the drastic cuts made to the text of the play. Many lines are acted or expressed nonverbally rather than spoken. Here is the way one critic summarizes these stylistic differences and their effect on the way we see and respond to Hamlet: "Olivier's direction emphasizes Hamlet's entrapment; close-ups stress his inwardness and long shots make him seem diminished and isolated in the context of Elsinore. Left to his own devices, Olivier's Hamlet would decline and die of grief. Gibson's Hamlet snarls; low-angle shots and vibrant close-ups make him dominate each moment on screen" (Keyishian, 78).

Analysis and Interpretation

1. Zeffirelli makes a number of cuts to Shakespeare's text to get his film down to a 135-minute running time. Make a list of key scenes or lines that Zeffirelli has cut from his screenplay. What does his strategy seem to be? What criteria has he used in deciding what to keep and what to cut? How does his editing strategy compare to Olivier's?

2. How does Zeffirelli's film portray Hamlet's relationships to his mother and to Ophelia? Does Gibson's Hamlet sexualize his relationships to women? To what extent do sexuality and femininity (or a fear of feminine sexuality) play a part in his character? How would you sketch out a feminist interpretation of Zeffirelli's film?

3. To what extent do you think Zeffirelli has succeeded in his goal of creating a more accessible and popular *Hamlet* for contemporary audiences? Do you think his film is understandable? What does it help you to see about Hamlet's character and motivations? Do you think the film would make sense for audiences who have not read the play? Is that important? Why?

4. Find examples of scenes that Zeffirelli has invented or added (like the funeral scene at the beginning, for example). Look at the way he stages the major soliloquies as well. How is his visual and narrative presentation different from Olivier's?

What effect do these differences have on your experience and understanding of the play?

Hamlet
Kenneth Branagh, Director, 1996

Kenneth Branagh—*Hamlet*	Charlton Heston—*Player King*
Derek Jacobi—*Claudius*	
Julie Christie—*Gertrude*	Rosemary Harris—*Player Queen*
Kate Winslet—*Ophelia*	
Michael Maloney—*Laertes*	Billy Crystal—*First Gravedigger*
Richard Briers—*Polonius*	
Nicholas Farrell—*Horatio*	Robin Williams—*Osric*
Timothy Spall—*Rosencrantz*	Gerard Depardieu—*Reynaldo*
Reece Dinsdale—*Guildenstern*	Jon Gielgud—*Priam*
	Judi Dench—*Hecuba*
Rufus Sewall—*Fortinbras*	Richard Attenborough—*English Ambassador*
Jack Lemmon—*Marcellus*	
Brian Blessed—*Ghost*	John Mills—*Old Norway*

If Zeffirelli's is a populist *Hamlet*, perhaps Branagh's film might be described as a purist's *Hamlet*. Branagh's 1996 film includes (almost) every line from Shakespeare's play, staying methodically close to the text (and including most of the disputed scenes), with very few cuts, abridgements, or rearrangements of scenes or even individual lines. As a result, Branagh's film runs 242 minutes, just over four hours. If you watch Branagh's film after Olivier's or Zeffirelli's, you'll be struck by the substantial differences, not only in the length and discursiveness of the scenes, but also in the feel and texture of the film as a whole. Branagh's film seems much more concerned with the political and social world surrounding Hamlet. Fortinbras and the approach of his army toward Elsinore tend to drive the plot along, and the modern-era military feel of the film is notably different from the medieval symbolism and psychology of both Olivier and Zeffirelli.

In genre terms, Branagh's film borrows much from the epic tradition of *Gone with the Wind*, *Ben Hur*, and *Doctor Zhivago*. This is in part simply a matter of length—at four hours, Branagh's *Hamlet* is inevitably a different kind of cinema experience than the two-hour adaptations of Olivier and Zeffirelli. As one critic describes, "Epic films tend to be paced majestically, prizing plenitude and variety over compactness and consistency of tone. Events tend to be broken up into episodes that are linked but self-contained, and enacted in a wide assortment of places" (Keyishian, 78). The sharp narrative focus of the Olivier and Zeffirelli versions of the play is sacrificed in Branagh's epic, but the abundance of Shakespeare's text and the rich intertextuality of the play are regained in exchange. Other film conventions typical of the epic are in evidence in Branagh's film as well. Flashbacks are used in several instances to show audiences visually what a character is remembering or retelling in a speech. The most notable examples of this are the flashbacks of Hamlet and Ophelia in bed together, making it explicit for audiences that the two have indeed been romantically and sexually involved.

If we have any doubts that Branagh's film draws on the conventions of the epic, his treatment of the "How all occasions do inform against me" soliloquy (4.4.34-67) should be enough to convince us. Branagh delivers the speech from a snowy, windswept mountain ridge, with a craggy rim of peaks behind him in the distance. The entire scene is white with snow and wind, and as he delivers the lines, the camera begins to pull back slowly from tight focus to extreme wide angle. By the end of the speech, Hamlet is a tiny black speck against a sweeping landscape of mountainous white. The visual tells us that whatever else he may be, Hamlet is but a man, a small piece in a very, very large world. Symphonic music rises, and as Hamlet delivers the final lines, the kettle drums throb—"My thoughts be bloody or be nothing worth!"—and we fade to black, then Intermission. This speech, deleted from many films and stage performances, becomes the centerpiece and turning point of Branagh's film, on both a dramatic and a cinematic level.

The set design and visual style of Branagh's film are markedly different from both Olivier and Zeffirelli as well. Branagh's Elsinore is the real-world Blenheim Palace, an eighteenth-century country house (residence of the Duke of Marlborough) that is opulent and splendidly wealthy. This choice dictates the costumes, which are nineteenth century and heavily militarized, with muskets and cannon as well as swords and rapiers. Blenheim is filled with mirrors, and Branagh even films the "To be or not to be" soliloquy with Hamlet standing in front of a mirror. The mirrors signal both self-consciousness and surveillance: In one scene, Hamlet confronts Ophelia, knowing that Polonius is watching from behind a mirrored door, even pressing her face into the two-way glass once he has opened and searched behind every door but one. Branagh's Elsinore is rich, gaudy, proud, and undeniably corrupt in its pursuit of conspicuous consumption.

An interesting visual device frames the film: At the beginning of the film, the camera lingers over the pedestal of a large stone statue of old King Hamlet. We return to this statue again at the end of the film, as Fortinbras's soldiers are tearing it down. The last image of the film is the head of King Hamlet as it tumbles from the statue. This visual device echoes not only Shelley's famous poem "Ozymandias," with its poignant recognition that even the greatest monuments of the greatest kings erode over eons of time, but also the toppling of Lenin statues all over Russia at the fall of the Soviet Union in 1989-90. Branagh seems to use this image to link his *Hamlet* to the larger cycles of human history and cyclic change, suggesting perhaps that another epoch of historical time is beginning with the rise of Fortinbras.

Analysis and Interpretation

1. Unlike any of the other *Hamlet* films, Branagh's film uses the complete Shakespeare text (with a few minor edits). Which scenes stand out for you when you watch this film alongside the others? How does your view of the play and its central dramas change with the inclusion of these scenes?

2. Critic Harry Keyishian writes of Branagh's use of epic conventions: "This *Hamlet*, to be sure, is not reflective of the early epic, which tends to celebrate national values and aspirations, but rather of a later, revisionist kind, full of subversive ironies and demythification" (80). What subversive ironies and demythification do you find in Branagh's film? How does it compare to a nationalistic history play like *Henry V*? How does Branagh manage to merge epic filmmaking with Shakespearean tragedy? Is his film still a tragedy, in either an Aristotelian or Shakespearean sense? Or has it become something different?

3. Besides the obvious symbolism of the large statue of King Hamlet that begins and ends the film, what other key visual symbols or motifs does Branagh use? Make a list of the key visual symbols and motifs you find, and compare them to Olivier's or Zeffirelli's. What differences do you find? What is their significance?

4. Here is how Kenneth Branagh himself describes his filmmaking strategy for *Hamlet*: "The screenplay is what one might call the 'verbal storyboard.' An inflexion of a subjective view of the play which has developed over the years. Its intention was to be both personal, with enormous attention paid to the intimate relations between the characters, and at the same time epic, with a sense of the country at large and of a dynasty in decay" (Behrens 786). What parts of the film are "intimate"? Which are "epic"? How do Branagh's strategies compare to those of other filmmakers? Is his juxtaposition of the personal and the political stories effective? Is it more authentic or "true" to the play? Why or why not?

5. Roger Ebert compared Branagh's *Hamlet* to Olivier's in a January 1997 review of the Branagh film: "Branagh's *Hamlet* lacks the narcissistic intensity of Laurence Olivier's, ... but the film as a whole is better, placing Hamlet in the larger context of royal politics, and making him less a subject for pity" (Behrens 788). Do you agree with Ebert's comparisons? What evidence from the two films supports his observations? What evidence might you use to construct a counterargument?

Hamlet
Michael Almereyda, Director, 2000

Ethan Hawke—*Hamlet*	Julia Stiles—*Ophelia*
Kyle MacLachlan—*Claudius*	Bill Murray—*Polonius*
Diane Venora—*Gertrude*	Karl Geary—*Horatio*
Liev Schreiber—*Laertes*	Sam Shepard—*The Ghost*

Michael Almereyda has been described as the archetypal 'indie' filmmaker, producing low-budget, art-house films outside of the major film studio circuit. His previous films include *Another Girl, Another Planet* (1994) and *Nadja* (1995), about a vampire in Manhattan. Both films were produced using toy cameras on miniscule budgets, and both became cult hits (Behrens 816). Almereyda seems to be in unusual company in the context of monumental greats like Laurence Olivier or massive studio budgets like those enjoyed by Kenneth Branagh. Yet his *Hamlet*, set in contemporary New York City and starring Ethan Hawke and Julia Stiles (who appears in other Shakespeare-based films including *10 Things I Hate about You* and *O*), is a haunting and effective take on *Hamlet* in a postmodern techno-thriller setting.

By setting the film in a present-day context, Almereyda is able to make explicit links between the corruption of the Danish court and the modern corporation. Denmark has become Denmark Corporation, with Kyle MacLachlan as CEO Claudius, challenged by renegade upstart Fortinbras. The proxy fight over the chairmanship of the corporation is chronicled in the pages of *USA Today*, pages Claudius ceremoniously rips to pieces before his assembled shareholders as he announces his new position and his new wife, Gertrude. Elsinore Castle becomes the Elsinore Hotel, complete with video surveillance cameras that capture images of the ghost of Hamlet's father (Sam Shepard) as he walks through the laundry room and across the balconies high above Times Square.

Most importantly, the contemporary setting allows Almereyda to introduce the theme of technology as a mediating force in human relationships. Hamlet, for example, is now a budding amateur filmmaker himself. Instead of the play within the play, in Almereyda's film we get a *film* within the play. *The Mousetrap* is "a film/video by Hamlet," and we see Hamlet at work editing and filming throughout the film. Several major soliloquies are spoken into the camera or replayed on a grainy digital monitor. Answering machines and faxes also serve as postmodern messengers in the film. Almereyda suggests the high degree to which all our interactions and communications are now mediated by machines. Hamlet even delivers his "get thee to a nunnery" speech to Ophelia via her answering machine.

Despite the high tech gadgets and the contemporary setting, Almereyda's film uses Shakespeare's original language throughout. It may strike some viewers as odd or jarring to hear Hamlet speaking Renaissance English while walking around modern Manhattan, but the effect in fact highlights the language and draws attention to the speech patterns effectively. In one tongue-in-cheek scene, Hamlet delivers his "To be or not to be" soliloquy as he wanders through the aisles of a Blockbuster video outlet. The product sign visible on the shelf behind him reads "ACTION."

Analysis and Interpretation

1. One reviewer of Almereyda's film, Alexandra Marshall, commented that Almereyda's women characters are deeper and more interesting than in any other filmed *Hamlet*. Marshall wrote: "Julia Stiles...embodies Ophelia with an authenticity equal to Diane Venora's Gertrude. In this film, we truly experience Ophelia's madness as the high-cost consequence of her insight. ... This Gertrude and Ophelia ... make us aware of how much of the story we have missed in less 'modernized' *Hamlet*s with their unexplored women" (Behrens 830-1). Compare the presentation of Gertrude and Ophelia in this film with those in the other three *Hamlet* films. What evidence do

you find to support Marshall's claim? What evidence might challenge or modify her assertions? Are the modern women characters stronger and more fully developed? In what ways? Which representation seems most satisfying to you?

2. Make a list of all the different uses and representations of technology and gadgetry in Almereyda's film. How do these devices function? What do they add to the story? Why?

3. Ethan Hawke is the youngest actor among the four who play Hamlet in the four films we've been discussing here. How does his performance compare to the others? Do you like his Hamlet? How would you describe his style? What sides of Hamlet's character does Hawke want to show us? Is his Hamlet more or less likable than the others? Why?

4. Notice how Almereyda's editing and cutting breaks up some of the scenes and interpolates them into other scenes. Sometimes a line or two from one scene repeats on a video monitor in the background or foreground of another live scene. How does this contemporary crosscutting method work? How does it both disrupt and support the dramatic narrative of the play?

Othello

Othello is Shakespeare's exploration of jealousy, specifically sexual jealousy, and its destructive power. In contrast to the broad scope and political contexts of *Hamlet*, the cast and scope of *Othello* are relatively small and its action is intensely focused on the three central characters, Othello, Iago, and Desdemona. Layered on to Shakespeare's exploration of the theme of sexual jealousy is a subtext focused on race. Iago uses Othello's blackness against him, suggesting that it would only be "natural" for a white woman like Desdemona to want the company of a man of her own race, following her "experiment" with a black husband and lover. The explicit racist language of some scenes has limited modern productions of the play or required radical rewriting in some cases. The narrative of the play depends heavily on the power of these racial stereotypes, however, both as they play on Othello's mind and as they circulate through the language of the play. One recent production actually foregrounds the issue of race of the play with a role reversal, in which Patrick Stewart plays a white Othello with an otherwise all black cast. Despite, or because of, its disturbing rhetoric, *Othello* continues to be relevant to modern audiences and contemporary concerns for racial and gender conflict.

Othello
Orson Welles, Director, 1952

Orson Welles—*Othello*	Hilton Edwards—*Brabantio*
Micheal MacLiammoir—*Iago*	Nicholas Bruce—*Lodovico*
	Michael Laurence—*Cassio*
Robert Coote—*Roderigo*	Fay Compton—*Emilia*
Suzanne Cloutier—*Desdemona*	Doris Dowling—*Bianca*

Orson Welles's 1952 production of *Othello* was remastered with restored sound and music tracks in 1992 and is now, fortunately for us, available on DVD. Filmed in Italy and Morocco in high-contrast black and white, the film is a powerful and poetic cinematic interpretation of Shakespeare's play. From its opening funeral procession scene, the film is taut and haunting, with a vibrant, incantatory vocal soundtrack. Welles uses repeated visual imagery suggesting cages, dungeons, and labyrinths to evoke the self-imposed isolation and confusion of Othello's mental landscape.

Welles uses some prose narration (voice-overs) to fill in the back story and make room for more intense coverage of key scenes. His camera work and editing suggest discontinuity and disruption, making heavy use of montage theories of layering and juxtaposition of images. As in other films, he makes use of low-angle shots to make figures loom menacingly over viewers. Rarely do we look down on Othello until the very last scene. Welles's visual style tends to dwell on the architecture of the Italian and Moroccan castles he uses for his sets; in one amazing scene, the

Cassio-Roderigo fight scene, the scene is filmed from a reflecting pool in a dramatic symmetry suggesting the artwork of M.C. Escher.

Othello
Oliver Parker, Director, 1995

Laurence Fishburne—*Othello*	Anna Patrick—*Emilia*
Irene Jacob—*Desdemona*	Nicholas Farrell—*Montano*
Kenneth Branagh—*Iago*	Indra Ove—*Bianca*
Nathaniel Parker—*Cassio*	Michael Sheen—*Lodovico*
Michael Maloney—*Roderigo*	Andre Oumansky—*Gratiano*

Contrary to popular belief, this most recent major film of *Othello* was not directed by Kenneth Branagh. Despite the powerful presence of Branagh in the film as Iago, the film was in fact directed by Oliver Parker. Parker's rich color, realistic sets, and more traditional camera work contrasts vividly with Orson Welles's heavily stylized and expressionistic version of the play. Laurence Fishburne gives a moving and deep performance as Othello, matching Branagh's sinister machinations as Iago.

Analysis and Interpretation

1. Compare the camera techniques of Welles and Parker. Notice the frequent use of low-angle shots and deep focus by Welles. How does this create an emotional effect for the film? How does Parker create a deeper sense of realism, in contrast to Welles's more artistic style?

2. How are the women portrayed in each film? Look carefully at Emilia's speech to Desdemona about women's capacity for unfaithfulness. Are the female characters stronger in one film than another? How are they different?

3. Both films cut lines and scenes to compress the length. What strategies do they use in making these cuts? Which one offers a more effective version of the play? Why?

4. Orson Welles is a white man playing Othello in blackface makeup. Laurence Fishburne is a popular African American actor, now known to screen audiences for his work in *The Matrix*. How are your perceptions of the main character, in part, responses to these actors and their performances? Is it possible for a white actor to give a convincing performance in a role like Othello? Is this question at all parallel to the issue of white artists performing hip-hop music? How about white audiences listening to hip-hop? How do contemporary debates about race in popular culture influence your interpretation of these two films? Would a white actor try to play Othello today? Why or why not?

CHAPTER 5

Additional Films and Projects for Writing and Research

The filmography in the back of this book lists most of the feature films based on Shakespeare plays that are currently available on DVD or VHS. Even this very selective listing includes 36 films. It's obviously not possible to present all of these films in detail in this short text. This chapter comments briefly on some of the more notable films of plays you may be likely to encounter in a college course. The questions at the end of each section are intended as starting points for discussion or writing about the films. The chapter ends with a list of suggested topics for writing and research.

Titus Andronicus

Titus (1999)

> Adapted from *Titus Andronicus*. Julie Taymor, director. Anthony Hopkins (Titus Andronicus), Jessica Lange (Tamora), Alan Cumming (Saturninus).

Titus Andronicus is perhaps Shakespeare's earliest tragedy, and it's certainly one of his most violent plays. It's probably not a play that would frequently appear on a college course syllabus. Nor are you likely to see it performed in summer Shakespeare festivals. But Julie Taymor's remarkable film is enough to propel readers to go back to the play with renewed interest. Taymor's work crosses between film and stage. She has won Tony awards for directing and costume design for her work on the Broadway production of *The Lion King*. Taymor has also directed a 1986 video-release version of *The Tempest* and a 1992 television production of *Oedipus Rex*.

The visual style of *Titus* is stunning, and it clearly shows the influence of Taymor's work on the stage. Many of the costumes are a stylized mixture of Roman, medieval, and punk elements. The sets offer both classical grandeur and post-apocalyptic decay. *Titus* is a feast for cinematography buffs; every single frame is aesthetically composed and polished to a decadent sheen. It remains to be seen whether Taymor's *Titus* will kick off a renaissance of interest in Shakespeare's Roman plays, but it certainly offers a brilliant example of the power of film to re-present one of his lesser-known dramas.

Analysis and Interpretation

1. One of the most notable things about *Titus* is its highly aestheticized presentation of violence. Does Taymor's aesthetic distance viewers from the impact of the violence of the play? Does the violence serve a purpose in the film? Does the film offer any hope for redemption or escape from the cyclical ritual of violence and retribution?

2. One critic writes, "The film production is marked by gross indulgence and hideous excess, but it is sometimes shockingly effective and even darkly humorous" (Welsh 101). What evidence of "dark humor" do you find in *Titus*?

3. What kinds of framing devices does Taymor employ in her film? How does the opening, where Lucius plays with his toy soldiers, function as a frame? What does Lucius discover or learn in the course of the film's story?

Macbeth

Macbeth (1948)

Orson Welles, director. Orson Welles (Macbeth), Jeanette Nolan (Lady Macbeth), Edgar Barrier (Banquo). (Black & White)

Macbeth (1971)

>Roman Polanski, director. Jon Finch (Macbeth), Francesca
>Annis (Lady Macbeth), Martin Shaw (Banquo).

Given the popularity of Shakespeare's "Scottish play," it's surprising that there have not been more feature films made based on *Macbeth*. Orson Welles's 1948 black-and-white version is a mixture of brilliant and inventive cinematography and low-budget production and editing. Welles reportedly was caught up in a dispute with the studio over the soundtrack, and the post-production work was redone without Welles's involvement. The film has been re-released with its original sound, in which the actors speak with a sometimes distracting Scottish accent. While it's clearly not the major achievement that Welles's *Othello* represents, this *Macbeth* is an intriguing, expressionistic rendition of the play from a powerful director.

Roman Polanski's 1971 *Macbeth* was financed by *Playboy* and marketed in part for its violence and nudity, a fact which has darkened its reputation among Shakespeare scholars ever since. Despite its bad reputation, Polanski's film is in fact very well made and vibrant. The weird sisters play an especially prominent role in the film. Contemporary audiences are unlikely to find its violence shocking, and, as Deborah Cartmell points out, violence is an integral part of Shakespearean theater (see her essay on violence in her book, *Interpreting Shakespeare on Screen*).

Analysis and Interpretation

1. These two versions of *Macbeth* are very different in their cinematic style and presentation. Welles's film is in black and white and uses a stylized, symbolic set; Polanski's aims for historical realism. How does this difference change the focus and impact of the story?

2. Lady Macbeth's role in Macbeth's tragedy has been one of the most interesting points of discussion among audiences for the play. How do these two films differ in their presentation of

Lady Macbeth? How are her role and influence interpreted differently by these two filmmakers?

King Lear

King Lear (1974)

> Edwin Sherin, director. James Earl Jones (King Lear), Raul Julia (Edmund), Paul Sorvino (Gloucester), Lee Chamberlin (Cordelia). (Made for TV)

King Lear (1984)

> Michael Elliott, director. Laurence Olivier (King Lear), Robert Lindsay (Edmund), Leo McKern (Gloucester), Anna Calder-Marshall (Cordelia). (Made for TV)

Ran (1985)

> Adapted from *King Lear*. Akira Kurosawa, director. Tatsuya Nakadai (Hidetora/Lear), Mieko Harada (Lady Kaede). (Japanese with English subtitles)

Two versions of *King Lear* have been filmed for television, and both are now available on DVD, but no recent feature films have been made of the play. If you can find copies in your college library, Grigori Kosintsev's *Karol Lir* (in Russian, 1970) and Peter Brook's 1971 production are both excellent.

1. Peter Brook once commented that *King Lear* is a play that is impossible to film. What about *Lear* would make a producer and filmmaker make such a comment? What problems do you think filmmakers would encounter in trying to translate *Lear* from the stage to the screen?

2. Most critics consider Akira Kurosawa's *Ran* to be the most successful and important filmed version of *Lear*, despite the fact that Kurosawa rewrites the play and changes the setting to

fedual Japan. What elements of Shakespeare's play does Kurosawa present, and how does he change the story? Do you consider his treatment to be effective? How does *Ran* demonstrate the cultural translatability of Shakespeare's play?

The Tempest

The Tempest (1991)

> Derek Jarman, director. Heathcote Williams (Prospero), Toyah Wilcox (Miranda).

Tempest (1982)

> Adapted from *The Tempest*. Paul Mazursky, director. John Cassavetes (Phillip), Gena Rowlands (Antonia), Raul Julia (Kalibanos), Molly Ringwald (Miranda).

Prospero's Books (1991)

> Adapted from *The Tempest*. Peter Greenaway, director. John Gielgud (Prospero), Michael Clark (Caliban), Isabelle Pasco (Miranda).

The Tempest has been more broadly and loosely adapted by filmmakers than most of the other plays discussed in *Screening Shakespeare*. It has been reworked as science-fiction space epic (*The Forbidden Planet*, 1956) and as a contemporary fable about an architect and his failing marriage in Paul Mazursky's 1982 film *Tempest*.

As one critic writes of Derek Jarman's adaptation: "Some purists may object to its campy extravagance, but its originality cannot be denied" (Welsh 97). Jarman's film combines a low-budget, avant-garde film style with a distinctively gay sensibility and camp aesthetic to produce a remarkable synthesis that is more an extended meditation on *The Tempest* than a cinema remake.

Compared to other films of the play, however, Jarman's "inventive and unconventional adaptation comes nearest to the play itself, even if the betrothal mask is oddly imagined and the text restructured and abridged" (Welsh 97).

Mazursky's *Tempest* is recast in modern English, but it retains a good bit of the story of *The Tempest* in outline form. John Cassavetes plays the Prospero-like role of Philip Dimitrius, a successful American architect going through a type of mid-life crisis. Dissatisfied with his life and career, Philip abandons Manhattan and his life as an architect and runs off to an Aegean island with his daughter Miranda (Molly Ringwald). Philip meets Aretha (an Ariel figure, played by Susan Sarandon), who gives up her nightclub singing job to accompany Philip and Miranda to the Greek island. Ironically, the very people Philip is trying to escape from later appear on his little island—his boss Alonzo, Philip's wife (Gena Rowlands), and Alonzo's son Freddie. While the modern language and realism shifts the focus of the play from Prospero (Philip) and his magic to his relationships with his wife and daughter, the themes of reconciliation and forgiveness closely mirrors the resolution of Shakespeare's play.

Peter Greenaway's creative adaptation focuses on the action of Prospero (John Gielgud) as he writes a play called *The Tempest*. The film is about the composition of the story as much as it tells the story itself. All lines are spoken by Gielgud; the rest of the characters are like puppets for his imagination. The film concludes as Prospero sits down to write *The Tempest*. The experience of watching the film is like having John Gielgud read the play to us as we watch the story unfold before our eyes, a magical puppet show taking place in the narrator's imagination.

Analysis and Interpretation

1. All three film adaptations of *The Tempest*, like the play itself, present a world that is a complex mixture of fantasy and reality. How does each film create a visual world to represent, cinematically, the island world of Shakespeare's play?

2. Each of these films, like Shakespeare's play, is in part a meditation on the power of fantasy and art. Who controls that power in each film? By what means? To what ends? Is that power always beneficent or can it also be malevolent?

3. Power, creativity, and sexuality seem to be closely interrelated in the world of *The Tempest*. How is this interrelationship presented in each of these films?

4. Some modern readers and critics have read *The Tempest* as a kind of allegory of colonialism. (Consult the bibliography in Bevington for specific references.) How do these films deal with the issue of Prospero and his power over and relationship with Caliban? Does their relationship change over the course of the film(s)? In what way?

Projects for Writing and Research

Focus on Directors. Choose one film director who has made several films based on Shakespeare's plays (Welles, Olivier, Zeffirelli, Branagh). Compare two or more films by this director in order to identify some characteristics of style, technique, and presentation that exemplify this director's work. What is unique and distinctive about this director's films? How do the films present a particular interpretation or viewpoint of the plays?

Focus on Reviews. Do some research to locate three or four reviews of a Shakespeare film that were published shortly after the film's release. (This project is especially interesting if you choose a film released prior to 1990.) Read and synthesize the reviews. Did reviewers agree about the qualities of the film? What did contemporary reviewers like and dislike about it? What aspects of the film were controversial? How do those reviews compare to more recent assessments of the film?

Focus on Adaptation. Shakespeare plays have often been "loosely" adapted, in both comic and tragic modes. Choose one recent adaptation (*10 Things I Hate About You*, *O*, or *Scotland, Pa*, for example) and write a critical analysis of the film as a remake of the Shakespeare play. How does the film translate Shakespeare into a different time and place? How effective is this translation?

Focus on a Scene. It can often be very helpful to choose a single scene from a play and compare its treatment in two or more different films. Choose one scene from a play you are interested in, and write a comparative analysis of two or more films' presentation of that scene. Pay attention to detail—look at camera movement and position, acting, and other elements of film technique. Write a detailed close reading of the scene, analyzing the key differences in the way each version is presented and the significance of those differences for your understanding of the scene.

Focus on Popular Culture. In addition to the Shakespeare plays themselves, most feature films also make many references to the popular culture of their times. This can happen through the presence of actors that audiences know from other films, the use of visual allusions to other texts or films, product placement, and any number of other cinematic echoes and allusions. (Think of Mel Gibson as Hamlet, for example, or the omnipresence of advertising logos in Luhrmann's *Romeo + Juliet.*) Write an analysis of the way a particular film draws upon and uses popular cultural imagery and references to reach an audience. What happens when Shakespeare is reinvented in the context of popular culture?

WORKS CITED

Behrens, Laurence, and Leonard J. Rosen. "Good Take, Sweet Prince: *Hamlet* on Film." *Writing and Reading Across the Curriculum*, 8th ed. New York: Longman, 2003. 711-843.

Bevington, David, ed. *The Complete Works of Shakespeare*, 5th ed. New York: Longman, 2004.

Bordwell, David, and Kristin Thompson. "The Power of *Mise-en-Scene*." *Film Art: An Introduction*. 6th ed. New York: McGraw-Hill, 2001. 157-74.

Cartmell, Deborah. *Interpreting Shakespeare on Screen*. New York: St. Martin's, 2000.

Frye, Northrop. *Anatomy of Criticism: Four Essays*. Princeton: Princeton UP, 1957.

Keyishian, Harry. "Shakespeare and Movie Genre: The Case of *Hamlet*." In Jackson, Russell, ed. *The Cambridge Companion to Shakespeare on Film*. Cambridge: Cambridge UP, 2000. 72-81.

Pearce, Craig, and Baz Luhrmann. *William Shakespeare's Romeo & Juliet: The Contemporary Film, The Classic Play*. New York: Bantam Doubleday Dell, 1996.

Welsh, James M., Richard Vela, and John C. Tibbetts, eds. *Shakespeare into Film*. New York: Checkmark Books, 2002.

ADDITIONAL RESOURCES

Shakespeare's Life and Works

Laroque, François. *The Age of Shakespeare.* Trans. Alexandra Campbell. New York: Harry N. Abrams, 1993.

A pocket-sized book for general readers, *The Age of Shakespeare* includes an impressive collection of images, many of which are in color. Typical period dress, architecture, and daily life, as well as famous paintings and historical documents, are presented in this readable and engaging book. Includes biographical information and images on Shakespeare, a discussion of the mythology of Queen Elizabeth, and a chapter on the changes occurring after the queen's death and the beginning of the Stuart period. A good source for historical background on England and Europe in 1600.

Dobson, Michael, and Stanley Wells, eds. *The Oxford Companion to Shakespeare.* Oxford: Oxford UP, 2001.

A collection of short alphabetical entries on characters, historical figures, literary sources, and actors who have played a part in Shakespeare's works and their subsequent history. Especially useful are the scene-by-scene plot synopses for the plays, which are a great help in locating specific scenes or events from the films. Wonderful black-and-white drawings and photos of key performers and performances.

Internet Resources

The Internet Movie Database. <http://us.imdb.com/>

> A comprehensive guide to films and the film industry. Can be searched by title, author, director, or actor. Provides complete cast and crew credits for all of the films discussed in *Screening Shakespeare,* as well as links to professional and user reviews.

Movie Review Query Engine. <http://www.mrqe.com>

> A search engine useful for finding reviews of specific films. Includes reviews of early as well as recent Shakespeare films, many contemporary with the films' release. Also includes reviews of DVD and VHS re-releases.

General Film Resources

Bordwell, David, and Kristin Thompson. *Film Art: An Introduction,* 6th ed. New York: McGraw-Hill, 2001.

> Bordwell and Thompson's readable textbook remains the most popular for college film courses. It is widely available in campus bookstores. The standard text in film analysis and history, *Film Art* features useful discussions of film history, film genres, major directors, and types of film theory and criticism. Includes a detailed bibliography of film resources and a helpful glossary of film terms.

Jill Nelmes, ed. *An Introduction to Film Studies,* 2nd ed. London: Routledge, 1999.

> This text offers a more theoretical take on film studies than Bordwell and Thompson. Includes very interesting chapters on the film industry and film technology, and a good if challenging introduction to contemporary feminist and psychoanalytic film theories.

Shakespeare and Film

Cartmell, Deborah. *Interpreting Shakespeare on Screen.* New York: St. Martin's, 2000.

> Cartmell's study is intended for college readers and takes a critical approach, looking at key issues in specific plays. Chapter 1 considers violence in *Macbeth* and *King Lear*; chapter 2, gender in *Hamlet*; chapter 3, sexuality in *Romeo and Juliet* and *Much Ado About Nothing*; chapter 4 race in *Othello* and *The Tempest*; and chapter 5 nationalism in *Henry V*. This book offers an important application of recent critical theory to the films and a strong argument for reading Shakespeare against the grain.

Davies, Anthony, and Stanley Wells, eds. *Shakespeare and the Moving Image: The Plays on Film and Television.* Cambridge: Cambridge UP, 1994.

> This volume gathers 14 academic essays on various topics related to the film and television versions of major plays. It provides especially good coverage of the tragedies (at least those filmed before 1994) and includes a selective filmography.

Jackson, Russel, ed. *The Cambridge Companion to Shakespeare on Film.* Cambridge: Cambridge UP, 2000.

> An interesting collection of 17 original essays on various aspects of Shakespeare film. The editor, Russel Jackson, has served as consultant to Kenneth Branagh and comments effectively on some of the key issues involved in translating the plays into film. Includes essays in four areas: adaptation, genre, directors, and critical issues (gender, race, nationalism). This is a fairly academic collection but useful for students and general readers who want to tackle some sophisticated approaches to the plays on film.

Jorgens, Jack J. *Shakespeare on Film*. Bloomington: Indiana UP, 1977. Rpt. Lanham, MD: University Press of America, 1991.

The first book-length critical survey of Shakespeare films, and still one of the most useful introductions to the serious study of the films. Includes a valuable essay on "Shakespeare and Nonverbal Expression" and detailed analyses of 16 films, focusing on the work of Welles, Polanski, Peter Brook, Franco Zeffirelli, Akira Kurosawa, and Russian director Grigori Kosintzev.

Rothwell, Kenneth S. *A History of Shakespeare on Screen: A Century of Film and Television*. Cambridge: Cambridge UP, 1999.

This book is a definitive history of Shakespeare in film and television. Rothwell generously narrates the evolution of Shakespearean cinema, providing context and background for individual plays. He includes a substantial if not exhaustive filmography as well. Sometimes his analysis of particular films slips into evaluation and critique, and at these points Rothwell can be both entertaining and provocative.

Welsh, James M., Richard Vela, and John C. Tibbetts, eds. *Shakespeare into Film*. New York: Checkmark Books, 2002.

This useful book combines a number of longish essays originally published in *Literature/Film Quarterly* with an encyclopedic compilation of alphabetical entries on each of the plays. This is a good starting point for any serious research project on Shakespeare and film, since it includes a history of both film and film criticism.

SELECT FILMOGRAPHY

This filmography includes feature films and adaptations of Shakespeare's plays. It is limited to films currently available on VHS or DVD. With a few exceptions, it does not include films made for television or films in languages other than English.

Entries are alphabetical by title. Adaptations are listed following the plays they are based upon. When more than one film is listed for a given play, the films are listed in chronological order.

If you are looking for additional films, or a more inclusive list of television or foreign films, I recommend searching the *Internet Movie Database*. Rothwell's *A History of Shakespeare on Screen* also includes a comprehensive filmography.

As You Like It (1936)

> Paul Czinner, director. Laurence Olivier (Orlando), Elisabeth Bergner (Rosalind). (Black & White)

Hamlet (1948)

> Laurence Olivier, director. Laurence Olivier (Hamlet), Basil Sydney (Claudius), Eileen Herlie (Gertrude), Jean Simmons (Ophelia). (Black & White)

Hamlet (1991)

> Franco Zeffirelli, director. Mel Gibson (Hamlet), Alan Bates (Claudius), Glenn Close (Gertrude), Helena Bonham Carter (Ophelia).

Hamlet (1996)

Kenneth Branagh, director. Kenneth Branagh (Hamlet), Derek Jacobi (Claudius), Julie Christie (Gertrude), Kate Winslet (Ophelia).

Hamlet (2000)

Michael Almereyda, director. Ethan Hawke (Hamlet), Kyle MacLachlan (Claudius), Diane Venora (Gertrude), Julia Stiles (Ophelia).

Henry V (1944)

Laurence Olivier, director. Laurence Olivier (King Henry V), Leslie Banks (Chorus), Renée Asheron (Katherine).

Henry V (1989)

Kenneth Branagh, director. Kenneth Branagh (King Henry V), Derek Jacobi (Chorus), Emma Thompson (Katherine).

Julius Caesar (1953)

Joseph L. Mankiewicz, director. Marlon Brando (Antony), James Mason (Brutus), John Gielgud (Cassius). (Black & White)

Julius Caesar (1970)

Stuart Burge, director. Charlton Heston (Antony), Jason Robards (Brutus), Richard Johnson (Cassius).

King Lear (1974)

Edwin Sherin, director. James Earl Jones (King Lear), Raul Julia (Edmund), Paul Sorvino (Gloucester), Lee Chamberlin (Cordelia). (Made for TV)

King Lear (1984)

> Michael Elliott, director. Laurence Olivier (King Lear), Robert Lindsay (Edmund), Leo McKern (Gloucester), Anna Calder-Marshall (Cordelia). (Made for TV)

Ran (1985)

> Adapted from *King Lear*. Akira Kurosawa, director. Tatsuya Nakadai (Hidetora/Lear), Mieko Harada (Lady Kaede). (Japanese with English subtitles)

Love's Labour's Lost (2000)

> Kenneth Branagh, director. Kenneth Branagh (Berowne), Alicia Silverstone (The Princess of France), Nathan Lane (Costard).

Macbeth (1948)

> Orson Welles, director. Orson Welles (Macbeth), Jeanette Nolan (Lady Macbeth), Edgar Barrier (Banquo). (Black & White)

Macbeth (1971)

> Roman Polanski, director. Jon Finch (Macbeth), Francesca Annis (Lady Macbeth), Martin Shaw (Banquo).

Kumonosu jo (Throne of Blood) (1957)

> Adapted from *Macbeth*. Akira Kurosawa, director. Toshirô Mifune (Washizu/Macbeth), Isuzu Yamada (Lady Washizu). (Black & White; Japanese with English subtitles)

Scotland, Pa. (2001)

> Adapted from *Macbeth*. Billy Morrisette, director. James LeGros (Joe 'Mac' McBeth), Maura Tierney (Pat McBeth), Christopher Walken (Lieutenant McDuff).

A Midsummer Night's Dream (1935)

> William Dieterle and Max Reinhardt, directors. James Cagney (Bottom), Mickey Rooney (Puck). (Black & White)

A Midsummer Night's Dream (1996)

> Adrian Noble, director. Lindsay Duncan (Hippolyta /Titania), Alex Jennings (Theseus/Oberon).

A Midsummer Night's Dream (1999)

> Michael Hoffman, director. Kevin Kline (Bottom), Michele Pfeiffer (Titania), Stanley Tucci (Puck).

Much Ado About Nothing (1993)

> Kenneth Branagh, director. Kenneth Branagh (Benedick), Emma Thompson (Beatrice).

Othello (1952)

> Orson Welles, director. Orson Welles (Othello), Micheál MacLiammóir (Iago), Robert Coote (Roderigo), Suzanne Cloutier (Desdamona). (Black & White)

Othello (1995)

> Oliver Parker, director. Laurence Fishburne (Othello), Kenneth Branagh (Iago), Irène Jacob (Desdamona), Nathaniel Parker (Cassio).

O (2001)

Adapted from *Othello*. Tim Blake Nelson, director. Mekhi Phifer (Odin James), Josh Hartnett (Hugo Goulding), Andrew Keegan (Michael Cassio), Julia Stiles (Desi Brable).

Richard III (1955)

Laurence Olivier, director. Laurence Olivier (Richard III), John Gielgud (Duke of Clarence), Claire Bloom (Lady Anne).

Richard III (1995)

Richard Loncraine, director. Ian McKellen (Richard III), Annette Bening (Queen Elizabeth), Kristin Scott Thomas (Lady Anne), Nigel Hawthorne (Duke of Clarence).

Romeo and Juliet (1968)

Franco Zeffirelli, director. Leonard Whiting (Romeo), Olivia Hussey (Juliet), John McEnery (Mercutio).

Romeo and Juliet (1996)

Baz Luhrmann, director. Leonardo DiCaprio (Romeo), Claire Danes (Juliet), Harold Perrineau Jr. (Mercutio).

The Taming of the Shrew (1929)

Sam Taylor, director. Mary Pickford (Katherine), Douglas Fairbanks (Petruchio). (Black & White)

The Taming of the Shrew (1967)

Franco Zeffirelli, director. Richard Burton (Petruchio), Elizabeth Taylor (Katharina).

10 Things I Hate About You (1999)

> Adapted from *The Taming of the Shrew*. Gil Junger, director. Heath Ledger (Patrick Verona), Julia Stiles (Katarina Stratford).

The Tempest (1991)

> Derek Jarman, director. Heathcote Williams (Prospero), Toyah Wilcox (Miranda).

Tempest (1982)

> Adapted from *The Tempest*. Paul Mazursky, director. John Cassavetes (Phillip), Gena Rowlands (Antonia), Raul Julia (Kalibanos), Molly Ringwald (Miranda).

Prospero's Books (1991)

> Adapted from *The Tempest*. Peter Greenaway, director. John Gielgud (Prospero), Michael Clark (Caliban), Isabelle Pasco (Miranda).

Titus (1999)

> Adapted from *Titus Andronicus*. Julie Taymor, director. Anthony Hopkins (Titus Andronicus), Jessica Lange (Tamora), Alan Cumming (Saturninus).

Twelfth Night; Or, What You Will (1996)

> Trevor Nunn, director. Helena Bonham Carter (Olivia), Nigel Hawthorne (Malvolio), Imogen Stubbs (Viola).

Notes

Notes